BIRDS:
KEEPING A
MIXED COLLECTION

BIRDS:
KEEPING A
MIXED COLLECTION

Irene Christie

Foreword by Rosemary Low

MEREHURST

LONDON

Cover photo: *The ultimate mixed collection – an aviary belonging to Raymond Sawyer, undisputed master of aviculture and owner of many mixed collections of birds. Seen in this picture are Black-winged Stilts and an African Pygmy Goose (photo by Cyril Laubscher)*

Published 1990 by Merehurst Limited
Ferry House
51/57 Lacy Road
London SW15 1PR

First published in 1985 under the title *Birds: a Guide to a Mixed Collection*

This edition © 1990 Merehurst Limited

ISBN 1 85391 106 2

Picture credits
Drawings by Linda Waters.
Photographs: Eric Barlow 58, 95 top, 100, 102, 135; *Cage and Aviary Birds* 24 top, 109, 112; Irene Christie 16, 17, 21, 24 bottom, 26 top, 27 top, 32, 38, 70, 85, 133; Michael Gilroy/Aquila Photographics 19 top, 22, 26 bottom, 27 bottom, 30 top, 37, 39, 40, 62, 65, 68, 76, 79, 82 top, 86, 87 bottom, 89, 90 top, 94, 98, 107, 117, 122, 134; A. C. Hughes Ltd 42; Cyril Laubscher 18 top, 31, 57, 64, 71, 80, 82 bottom, 83, 90 bottom left, 90 bottom right, 91, 95 bottom, 110, 114, 121, 125, 126, 128, 130, 139; Joe Mitchell 23 bottom, 59; Michael Plose 19 bottom, 30 bottom, 61, 118, 124, 131, 137; Colin Waterman 87 top, 119; Zoological Society of London 60, 67, 93, 97, 104, 106.

The author and publishers, together with Cyril Laubscher, wish to thank the following people for their help in making this edition possible by allowing their birds to be photographed: Paul and June Bailey, Trevor Bonneywell, Alan Donnelly, Phil Holland, Ron James, Ken Lawrence, Stanley Maughan, Doug Neill, Ron Oxley, Brian Pettitt, Mike and Jane Pickering, Val Read, Raymond Sawyer, Charlie Smith, Joyce Venner, Frank Wagner.

The publishers would also like to express their gratitude to all those whose birds were photographed for the first edition and also appear in this book; special thanks are also due to Ken Denham, who acted as Consultant Editor for the first edition.

Editor Lesley Young
Designed by Carole Perks
Typesetting by Deltatype Ltd

Reprographics by Fotographics Ltd, London–Hong Kong
Printed in Portugal by Printer Portuguesa
   Industria Grafica LDA

CONTENTS

FOREWORD

Exactly what is a mixed collection of birds? It could be defined as an aviary or series of aviaries containing examples from all or some of the most popularly kept groups of aviary birds: seedeaters, softbills, members of the parrot family, doves and quail. A typical mixed aviary might contain six to 12 pairs of seedeaters (such as grassfinches, waxbills and mannikins) and a pair each of Pekin Robins and Zosterops (representing the softbills), Splendid Grass Parrakeets, Diamond Doves and Chinese Painted Quail. This would be a sensible starting point for the beginner.

The aviary itself should be a modest and practical, but not inexpensive, construction, preferably sited near the owner's house where the busy antics of the occupants will provide hours of entertainment. Mixed aviaries come in many shapes and forms. The ultimate, in my opinion, is one which spans 6,070 sq m (1 1/3 acres) and has a height of 19.5 m (64 ft). This is Miami Metrozoo's unique walk-through aviary, known as the Wings of Asia. Here one can watch birds under conditions which reproduce their natural habitat, including a hardwood forest and a swamp. You need binoculars to observe some of the inhabitants!

No private aviculturist can hope to emulate such an ambitious and expensive project. But he or she can do much to make the birds' living conditions pleasant and comfortable and to take care of the requirements of the species whose habits or diet differ in small yet significant ways from those of the majority of the birds kept. The beginner has a lot to learn – as does the aviculturist with a lifetime's experience.

How can we learn more about our birds? There are two principal ways: observation, and reading and discussion. Observation is endlessly fascinating, especially in a mixed aviary, but it cannot teach us all we need to know. Books, on the other hand, can provide answers to many points which are a matter of mystery to the beginner. Which birds can I keep together? Are they hardy? Can I expect them to breed? Which plants are suitable for my aviary? The answers to these questions and many more can be found within these very readable pages.

There is much valuable advice on all aspects of maintenance of the birds and their accommodation. This book is a useful introduction to the beginner who is advised not to start too ambitiously. If he or she builds up a collection gradually, commencing with the hardier and less expensive species, disappointments will be fewer and enjoyment greater. Every year more and more people discover the joys of keeping birds. For many of these, Irene Christie's book will help to set them firmly on the path to their adventures with birds. Along the way there will be joys and inevitably there will be sadness. But there will never be a dull moment!

ROSEMARY LOW
LAS PALMAS, 1989

INTRODUCTION

One of the most challenging and rewarding types of bird keeping (aviculture for the purist), is the developing and maintaining of a mixed collection.

Wide ranging choices are involved, in types of birds, number and size of birds, not to mention accommodation. Then there is the decision of whether or not to attempt breeding. Perhaps you want a collection of really good songsters or birds of beautiful colours? The permutations are endless.

There is even a certain amount of controversy over which birds will agree together most harmoniously. Generally, no two 'bird experts' will completely agree on exactly the same birds for perfect harmony in a mixed group.

The selection of available birds also varies tremendously even from year to year. This year's rarity may become commonplace in next to no time.

Such factors are part of the mystique of forming a mixed collection and contribute greatly to the excitement. I found the challenge both stimulating and intriguing.

I also enjoyed comparing notes with fellow fanciers on their mixed collections and was often surprised to find groups of birds that in theory should not have been living in great harmony.

Keeping a mixed collection does involve a certain amount of experiment by trial and error. While I cannot provide the perfect recipe, I hope the ideas, hints and suggestions in this volume will give you a starting point.

I found great joy in building up a mixed collection, I hope you will too.

IRENE CHRISTIE

1
THE AVIARY

Most fanciers start out with the odd pair of birds, or even just one, but bird keeping has a tendency to develop far beyond one's original intentions. Sooner or later most serious fanciers opt for either an outdoor or indoor aviary to house their growing bird collection adequately.

All birds live healthily and contentedly in captivity for much longer if they can exercise their wings frequently. This prevents birds from becoming overweight and sluggish. In the wild, birds forage actively for their food, but captive birds have no such need. Their diet, rich in all the necessary ingredients, is readily available, provided by a thoughtful owner who may not at first realise that this can create problems.

Aviaries offer better conditions for birds than cages, as the aviary allows plenty of exercise. If keeping pairs of birds for breeding, it is essential to allow the maximum amount of space for flying, nesting, roosting and feeding.

Keeping pairs of birds in mixed collections may lead to squabbles, particularly when birds come into breeding condition. For this reason, it is important to select birds carefully. No such problem occurs if only cock birds of different species are kept together. Indeed many fanciers do just this, choosing them for their colourful plumage or singing ability. However, much depends on the individual nature of the birds concerned, as those of a placid nature mingle well even in small quarters.

THE OUTDOOR AVIARY

Outdoor accommodation for birds consists of a shelter or bird room for roosting and a flight for exercise. It should be planned so as to allow easy entrance for the owner with minimum disturbance and so that the birds can be locked in at night or during bad weather. The spot chosen should offer the maximum in light and fresh air, with protection from wet, cold or windy weather and also from excessive heat.

The shelter is the most important part of the aviary and needs to be designed with care to ensure that the owner can feed and maintain birds with minimum effort. The shelter must be damp- and

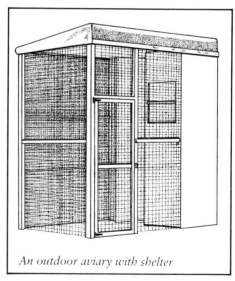

An outdoor aviary with shelter

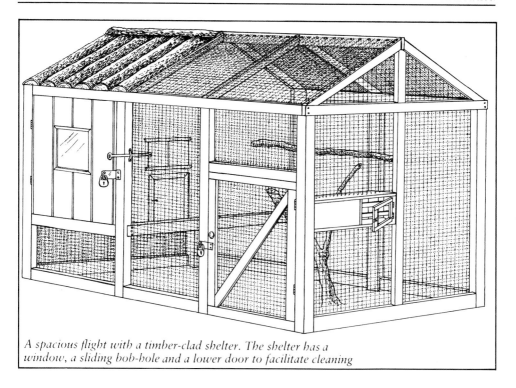

A spacious flight with a timber-clad shelter. The shelter has a window, a sliding bob-hole and a lower door to facilitate cleaning

draught-proof, yet with sufficient ventilation to give the birds ample supplies of fresh air during hot summer weather. A shelter built above ground level gives the greatest protection from vermin and damp.

The flight is constructed from wire mesh netting. The mesh must be small enough to prevent the birds from escaping and mice and other vermin from entering.

When using glass in the flight or shelter, it is most important to cover the inside with mesh netting, for birds can easily fly into glass and injure or kill themselves.

Height is important in an aviary since most birds like to fly up, and usually favour the highest possible position for roosting. To encourage the birds to roost under cover, the highest roosting point should be located inside the shelter. Also take into account that at times it is necessary to catch birds with a net. An extra high aviary may be needed if very large species are to be kept.

The space available often dictates the size of aviary. A large aviary allows the enthusiast to add to the collection without overcrowding and without having to re-plan or alter the original accommodation.

Length is the next most significant consideration. As great a length as possible should be allowed. Width is not as important, but from the point of view of appearance, the proportions should be well balanced.

How to sink a wire netting border

Drainage in the flight is very important. If your soil has good natural drainage, a normal earth floor topped up with fine grade gravel and perhaps a little freshly washed river sand is sufficient. Alternatively, turf may be laid, which should be allowed to settle well before birds are introduced to the aviary.

The floor of the aviary flight should be either concrete or paving stones for maximum ease of cleaning, or else natural earth or grass. If the aviary is not being planted out, plants in pots or tubs may be substituted to provide foliage. The floor of the shelter should be concrete or, for more warmth, concrete lined with timber.

Concrete flooring may be more expensive, but it is easy to keep clean and maintain Even if a soil floor is preferred, the walls surrounding the flight and shelter should be of cement with the founda-

tions taken to a depth of at least 46 cm (18 in). The walls should slope away from the base to give good drainage. This also prevents mice, rats and other vermin from digging their way in. Concrete flooring should be sloped to give drainage and protection in the same way. It may be hosed for ease of cleaning. Concrete floors may be covered with a layer of sand. Occasionally, fanciers use woodd shavings but the dust from these can cause eye infections in birds. Sand and peat moss are useful floor coverings to protect birds from damp and to absorb droppings. Earth floors should be forked over at least once a year and the top dressed with lime and fresh sand.

In countries with a hot climate, where earth floors are practical, the dry weather provides birds with an opportunity to dust bathe when the soil becomes dry and powdery. A dry floor is an important requirement for birds since chilling can be very harmful. Species, such as quail, which spend a lot of time on the ground, are the most susceptible.

To try to prevent cats from walking over the roof of the aviary and frightening the birds, suspend plastic mesh netting, stretched fairly tight, about 23 cm (9 in) above the roof. This is kinder than using barbed wire or broken glass which may cause injury to animals.

The most dangerous predators are usually rodents. Careful precautions must be taken and a concrete floored aviary is fairly easy to protect. For peace of mind, take the depth of concrete under the aviary and shelter floor to as much as 76 cm (30 in). Woodwork is vulnerable to rodents: once they start trying to gnaw their way in, they often return to complete the job, night after night. If the aviary has an earth floor, wire netting borders should be sunk to a depth of at least 61 cm (24 in) below the ground. The trench must be deep and wide enough to enable the wire netting to be bent outwards. Broken glass can be buried in the trench on the outside of the wire to discourage burrowing.

While mice are not quite as dangerous, they are undesirable. They are also able to get through mesh even of a very small diameter. They often frighten birds who may fly into shelter walls or flight wire and injure or kill themselves. If birds are sitting, they may be frightened off their nests and desert their young. If mice get into nests, they can injure the young unfledged birds, tumble them out of the nest or eat them. Mice droppings may contaminate bird food. To stop mice

from entering the flight or shelter, surround the base area with glass or sheet metal at least 30 cm (12 in) to 51 cm (20 in) in depth. Food dishes should be sited above ground level to avoid mice droppings or other contamination. This is not possible when keeping ground birds, such as species of quail.

Aviaries should be built with a low door or safety porch to prevent birds escaping when their owner enters. Doors may be fitted with springs to ensure speedy, efficient closure.

Electric lighting is indispensable. It enables the owner to check the birds on dark evenings, lock them away for the night, do any necessary chores and make sure there are no prowling cats or other predators in the vicinity. Automatic time-

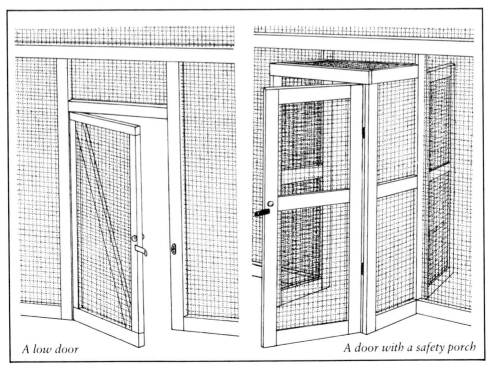

A low door

A door with a safety porch

controlled dimmer switches are recommended, because birds dislike a change from light to sudden darkness and often panic if the light is not reduced gradually. To prevent birds from burning themselves surround each bulb with a wire mesh screen several inches from its surface.

Birds only feed in the light. In some areas, it is advisable to switch on the lights for extra hours in winter, particularly in the morning, to give more feeding time. This is particularly important if birds are breeding in winter as they must be able to feed their chicks in the light.

The next question is that of warmth. The shelter should be well insulated from damp and draughts. In exposed areas, the flight may be protected from harsh winds by placing boards on one or more of its sides. Part of the roof may also be covered by placing green plasti-glass or similar material at a sloping angle to allow rain to run off easily. Many birds enjoy sitting in fine rain, which is good for their plumage, but most try to retreat from a heavy downpour.

In cold areas, the maximum temperature recommended for bird shelters or rooms is 15°C (60°F), since a higher temperature is not only costly to maintain, but is likely to weaken the birds. Radiators, hot water pipes and thermostatically controlled tubular heaters or fans may be used in the shelter. Some fanciers use oil or calor gas heaters, but these are not recommended since they can give off fumes which can make birds ill. There is also a risk of fire. Some birds winter successfully in a shelter that is dry and damp-proof without any extra heat, but others benefit from a little help as the nights turn frosty. A light bulb may often be sufficient. If in doubt, it is better to

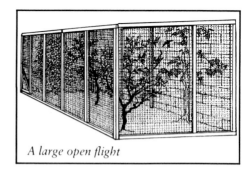

A large open flight

keep the birds a little warmer than necessary, as heat may be gradually reduced later. This is easier than treating a bird with pneumonia.

Many birds enjoy basking in sunshine in the morning light, so, if possible, the flight should be positioned to catch the morning sun rays. In warm climates, the afternoon sun may be too hot, so provide plenty of shade and cool, such as bushes, trees, water fountains, sprays and small pools. Pools must be shallow, so that young or small birds do not drown.

Humidity should be provided in the shelter to prevent the plumage drying out and becoming brittle. A small portable humidifier running on electricity may be used, or try placing a pan of boiling water in the shelter each day. Do make sure that the saucepan is covered with a net. A constant circulation of fresh air may be maintained by a low inlet, which should be proofed against mice, and an air outlet on the opposite wall of the shelter, high up under the eaves. These should be located away from perching birds, so that they are not caught in a draught.

In summer, the windows of the shelter or bird house may be left open and covered with wire netting. Do not leave them open at night unless the shelter is protected from invaders.

The shelter should be as light as possible to encourage birds to enter. The entry hole, or 'bobhole' should be high up. A further, larger door may surround the bobhole, to be opened in fine weather or at the owner's convenience. A sliding bobhole is often a good idea for shutting the birds in at night with ease.

Wire netting comes in a variety of sizes and weights and the mesh chosen varies according to the types of birds to be housed. Fanciers often paint the netting with black, lead-free enamel, making the birds easier to view. Welded wire mesh is more expensive than ordinary aviary wire netting, but is neater when finished, is easier to work on and lasts longer.

Ready-made aviaries of many different shapes and sizes may be purchased complete or in sectional panels from specialist suppliers. However, a home-designed and built structure can be tailor-made to requirements. First, measure the area available and decide how large the flight and shelter are to be. Using some graph paper, draw up a scale plan of the ground area and then draw both front and rear views of the accommodation to scale. Simple drawings are sufficient to check all measurements.

A lean-to aviary against a garden or house wall, comprising flight and shelter, is one of the most popular styles. A strong, sloping roof may be constructed from timber which should be given a weatherproof coating. The roof may be entirely of timber or half netting and half timber.

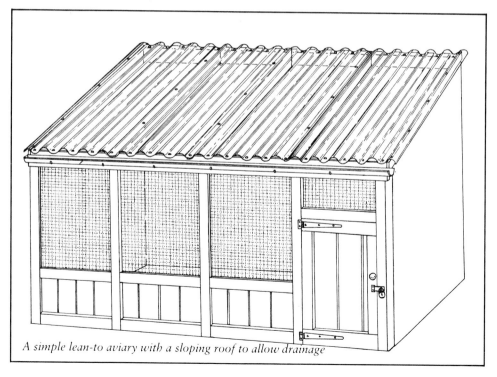

A simple lean-to aviary with a sloping roof to allow drainage

Circular and octagonal aviaries give a good all-round view of the birds, but generally rectangular or square structures utilise available space far more effectively and economically.

All timbers used in aviary construction should be treated with creosote to prevent mites and other infestation. This treatment also prevents wood from rotting due to damp and, once dry, creosote does not affect the occupants.

There are many alarm systems that can help to protect valuable birds against theft.

THE INDOOR AVIARY

Careful planning is needed for the indoor aviary to make sure it is suitable for birds, easy to clean and maintain. Depending on the type of birds to be kept, there are many different forms of indoor flight which the prospective fancier can purchase or construct himself.

Small softbills or seedeaters may be housed in a flight with a glass front, perhaps built into an alcove or chimney breast. If a spare room is available, it is a simple matter to construct a floor-to-ceiling wire mesh flight. The base may be made of wood in the form of a tray covered with a material which is easy to clean, and lined with frequently changed newspaper. To prevent seed husks from travelling outside the flight area, fix plastic sheeting across the lower half of the flight.

When keeping birds indoors, give their quarters a weekly spray with a good quality anti-mite preparation, paying particular attention to ends of perches and woodwork of any kind. Mites can be more troublesome indoors than in an outside aviary. Try to encourage the

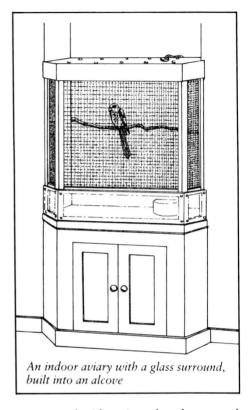

An indoor aviary with a glass surround, built into an alcove

presence of spiders since they destroy red mites. There should be no problems with mice and other vermin. In warm summer weather, strict cleanliness must be observed with regard to food and droppings, particularly if keeping softbills, since flies are encouraged if hygiene is neglected.

Keeping birds indoors creates more chores about the house. The birds need regular spraying with a hand spray containing warm water or else a bird bath in order to maintain good plumage. This aspect of their care must not be neglected, or feathers become dry and brittle. Preening is an activity which is undertaken by birds as part of their daily routine to distribute oil from their oil gland through their feathers. Without regular preening, feathers soon lose their lustre and sheen. A good spray or bath always encourages a bird to preen actively. Some birds enjoy a dust bath and a tray may be filled with a mixture of fine soil and sand for this purpose.

PLANTS

Once the aviary has been built the next step is to choose plants to enhance even

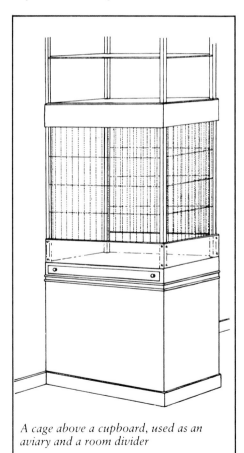

An indoor aviary on a window ledge which allows the window to be opened in suitable weather

A cage above a cupboard, used as an aviary and a room divider

the most simple aviary. These may be planted out or placed in troughs, planters and tubs in selected areas.

Many species are encouraged to breed by the shelter and seclusion of a densely planted aviary. Plants also attract insects, which the birds are able to catch and eat.

Climbing plants, such as vines and roses, are useful as a covering for aviary netting, giving shade and a pleasing appearance. However, beware of any plants with thorns or spikes which may create difficulties for you when catching birds.

Some birds, particularly the parrotlike species, may damage plants with their beaks. Laurel and rhododendron are both poisonous to budgerigars and parrakeets and so must never be included. It may be necessary to clean some of the plants occasionally if they are soiled with droppings, though generally normal rainfall will wash away any mess.

The following is a list of trees and plants which are safe to include in an aviary.

BERBERIS(*Mahonia aquifolum*)

An evergreen shrub which grows quickly and spreads well. It bears yellow flowers which fruit into blackish-blue, satin-like berries. The leaves turn dark, almost purple in winter months. Another variety of Berberis (*Mahonia hortorum*) is very similar with the same berries but grows to a greater height.

An indoor planted flight with a brick surround

BLACKBERRY (*Rubus fructicosus*)

A hardy species which does well in any type of soil, but prefers damp, shady conditions. It is a fast-growing bush which spreads very well. Birds love the luscious dark fruit and many insects are also attracted by it.

BOX (*Buxus sempervirens*)

A useful hedging shrub, preferred by small waxbills for nesting. It may be trimmed neatly for nesting birds during the breeding season but left to grow freely for shelter at other times. A very practical evergreen which flourishes in all soils in sun or shade.

CONIFER

There are numerous types of conifers suitable for aviaries. They have a pleasing appearance and tough foliage which withstands the attentions of small beaks. Dwarf conifers come in many different shapes and sizes and leaf colour. Many are, in fact, quite large and grow rapidly. Two recommended ones are:

NANA (*Picea mariana*) Dwarf Conifer

A slow-growing, compact, round-shaped spruce with blue-grey foliage. Birds, especially small finches, love climbing about in this. Like most of the conifer family, it prefers sandy soil and is very hardy.

LITTLE GEM (*Picea abies*) Dwarf Conifer

This grows in an attractive, dense, round green ball and attracts red spider mites, which are enjoyed by many birds. It grows well in sandy soil.

COTONEASTER (*Cotoneaster horizontalis and rotundifolia*)

The *Cotoneaster horizontalis* is a lovely

Inside a densely planted flight showing a selection of nest sites

spreading plant which looks very attractive with its pinky-white flowers. The *Cotoneaster rotundifolia* grows upright and has larger blossoms. Both types produce red berries and require a sunny area which is not too wet. The foliage lasts all the year round and are therefore very suitable plants to grow in an aviary in any garden.

ENGLISH HOLLY (*Ilex aquifolium*) or AMERICAN HOLLY (*Ilex opeca*)

Holly requires a sunny area but soil that is not too dry. Male and female bushes should be obtained if possible and planted side by side to ensure a mass of lovely bright red berries. Holly may be used for hedging, particularly the *pyramidalis* variety, which provides useful nesting sites. This species also produces plenty of fruit.

ENGLISH IVY (*Hedera helix*)

A very useful, attractive climber suitable for covering aviary netting or walls. Too much sun makes this plant shrivel. It prefers a shady spot. The evergreen colour is maintained throughout the year. The tiny flowers produce black berries which are occasionally eaten by birds. There is a larger-leaved variety called Hibernica which is also attractive.

Left: *an Orange-Cheeked Waxbill*
Far left: *a Purple Sugarbird cock*
Below: *an Indian Zosterops*

EUROPEAN ELDERBERRY (*Sambucus nigra*) or **COMMON ELDERBERRY** (*Sambucus canadensis*) or **RED ELDERBERRY** (*Sambucus pubens*)
Grows rapidly in most types of soil with sufficient humus. It needs plenty of sun and moisture to produce lush clumps of berries eagerly devoured by birds. The berries also attract insects to tempt the insect-eating species. It is easy to grow and maintain.

FORSYTHIA (*Forsythia spectabilis*)
The tough woody stems are impervious to beaks, and the profusion of yellow flowers makes a beautiful sight. It provides good shade, cover and useful nesting sites.

HAWTHORN (*Crataegus monogyna*)
A fairly tall tree which is very suitable for nesting purposes. It bears pleasantly scented, pinky-red flowers which produce bright red berries. These are enjoyed by many species of birds. Hawthorn does well in most soils in a sunny area.

HONEYSUCKLE (*Lonicera*)
A versatile climbing plant which looks very attractive and provides useful nesting sites. The lush flowers smell delicious and attract insects as well.

JUNIPER
Junipers are recommended and there are a great number from which to choose. One of the most attractive is:

BLUE STAR (*Juniperus squamata*)
An adaptable and hardy Juniper, the steel blue foliage is attractive. It grows very quickly and occasionally needs to be trimmed. In three years, this Juniper can grow to four times its original size.

MOCK ORANGE BLOSSOM (*Philadelphus coronarius*)
This delightfully scented shrub can grow very tall. A good choice as the blooms attract plenty of insects. It is a very hardy plant.

RASPBERRY (*Rubus*)
This needs similar conditions to the Blackberry. The rich, red fruit is also loved by birds.

RUSSIAN VINE (*Polygonum*)
Another very popular, rampant climbing plant suitable for aviaries. It rapidly covers aviary netting.

SNOWBERRY (*Symphoricarpus abus*)
A hardy, bushy shrub which bears a profusion of pink blossom and fruits into white berries, which are much appreciated by the small species of quail.

WEEPING WILLOW (*Salix babylonica*)
If plenty of space is available and waterfowl are kept on a small pond or lake, then reeds, rushes and this willow are very attractive.

WILD ROSE (*Rosa multiflora*)
There are many different varieties of wild rose. All make excellent and picturesque climbing plants for aviaries. They may also be used as nesting sites and they invite large numbers of useful insects. Sunny areas and damp soil are favoured.

PERCHES
These should vary in thickness to exercise the birds' feet properly. Dowel perching may be bought in pet stores and cut into various lengths as required. Natural perching should also be provided in the form of branches of different sizes. Incorrect

A planted aviary housing Diamond Sparrows and Zebra Finches

perches often cause birds' toenails to grow too long and curve into uncomfortable shapes. Metal perches should never be used. Some of the perches should be sited quite high up, particularly in the shelter for roosting. These should be the thinnest perches, which birds usually prefer.

Softbilled birds wipe their beaks on perches constantly, so natural perches should be replaced frequently, while dowel perches are easy to wash. Birds also foul their perches with droppings and dirty perches must always be replaced or washed. Many birds enjoy stripping the bark from branches and for this purpose, apple wood is a very good choice.

FEEDING DISHES AND DRINKERS

Feeding dishes should be placed where they are not fouled by bird droppings.

Different containers are required for various types of birds. Seedeaters need a dish which is fairly deep for mixed millets and plain canary seed. If several different dishes for millets and a separate one for canary seed are provided, it is possible to identify the birds' preference and balance their diet. Further containers should hold mineral grit, canary song food and insectile mixtures, dietary supplements and any other favoured snacks, such as apple, which some seedeaters really enjoy.

Food and water dishes may be made of china, earthenware, glass or plastic and should be scalded before use. Metal containers are often used for parrotlike species. Dietary supplements should not be given in metal containers because a chemical reaction may take place. Automatic bird seed feeders, which are efficient and reliable, may be purchased at pet stores.

Clear plastic or glass drinkers of tubu-

Left: *a Lavender Finch*
Above: *a Violet-Eared Waxbill*
Below: *a group of Masked Grassfinches*

A useful, seed-saving hopper

BIRD BATHS AND POOLS

The type of bird bath normally purchased for a garden can look very attractive within an aviary. Water pumps may be used to provide a fountain which can be another pleasing feature, but it may take some birds a little time to become accustomed to it. Bird baths and pools should always be shallow to avoid young birds drowning. The type of plastic pool normally used for small fish can be used if stones are placed on the bottom of the pool to reduce the depth. Baths and pools should have clean, clear water at all times and never be allowed to stagnate. If possible, provide fresh running water.

NESTING BOXES AND BASKETS

Nest boxes for finches, with a round entrance or a half square front, should be positioned at varying heights in the aviary. Cover should be given in the form of bundles of reeds, branches, heather, hedging screens, tree bark or shrubs. Wicker nest baskets come in various shapes with entrance holes in different positions, but need to be sprayed regularly with mild disinfectant as they attract

lar design keep water fresh and clean, although some birds tend to use them as shower baths. These are essential for nectar-feeding softbills. Any algae forming on the inside must be removed by regular, thorough cleaning.

Several feeding positions in an aviary prevent any squabbling or bullying over meals.

It is always better to place food above ground level, except for quail and other ground dwellers. Wild bird feeders on stands keep food in a clean condition well above the ground.

An easily constructed wooden case, suitable for carrying drinking tubes

mites and other tiny insects. A mild disinfectant will not cause any harm to the birds.

Some species favour canary nest pans or nest logs. The greater the variety of nest sites offered, the better the chance of birds attempting to breed. Coconut shells may be wired together to make an unusual nesting site for small finches. Care must be taken to ensure there is nothing for the birds to catch their feet on. Bundles of hay and dried grasses may be packed into mesh bags and hung up for the use of nesting birds.

Parrakeets and cockatiels need larger nest boxes and logs than smaller birds, although cockatiels use a budgerigar nest box quite frequently. It is often surprising how small a box some birds select if they are keen to breed. Perhaps a small box creates a feeling of security.

WIRED-IN SAFETY DOOR

A wired-in safety door is essential to prevent birds escaping. This should also allow the owner to feed the birds without entering the aviary, thus creating a minimum of disturbance.

OTHER SUNDRY EQUIPMENT

RACKS for green food
CLIPS for hanging up cuttlefish bone
BINS for seed storage
CATCHING NET
BROOM
CLEANING UTENSILS including a scraper for removal of droppings
TRAVEL CAGE
BIRD BATH CAGE
HAND MIST SPRAY
FIRST AID BOX This should contain such items as hydrogen peroxide to stop bleeding, cotton wool, disinfectant and nail clippers. A torch is another useful item.
HOSPITAL CAGE Used to provide sick birds with controlled heat. This can be a simple box cage with a light bulb fitted inside. Ensure it has adequate ventilation.
INCUBATOR Used for hatching eggs. There are many excellent makes available from specialist suppliers.

Right: *a Plum-Headed Parrakeet*
Below: *Peter's Twinspot*

Right: *a silver mutation of the Chinese Painted Quail*
Below: *a Pin-Tailed Parrot Finch*

2
FEEDING

orrect nutrition is one of the most important factors for healthy and contented birds. In the case of seedeaters, the seed diet is straightforward. The softbill fancier must take extra care, since the requirements of the many species of softbill are more exacting than those of seedeaters.

It is always worth while making that little extra effort to provide as wide a variety of food as possible. Additional nutrition and favoured tit-bits make the difference between the average healthy bird and the specimen with excellent show potential that is also eager to breed.

In general, hot weather causes the most problems with regard to following hygienic feeding routines. With nectar-feeding softbills, however, cold weather is a nuisance if severe enough to freeze the nectar mixture in its plastic tubes.

All birds require the following:

Vitamin A Promotes healthy skin and feathers and is essential for young birds.
Vitamin B Needed for the central nervous system and vitality.
Vitamin C Prevents skin disease.
Vitamin D Aids formation of bones.
Vitamin E Prevents sterility and aids fertility.

DIET FOR SEEDEATING BIRDS

Dry bird seed normally provides a satisfactory diet, but many experienced fanciers maintain that a diet of soaked and sprouted seed proves more nutritious. Cheap seed should be avoided since it usually contains a great deal of dust and proves difficult to germinate. Birds with young must be provided with ample quantities of good quality soaked and sprouted seeds. The vitamin content of sprouted seed is extremely high. Seeds should be soaked in cold water for 24 hours, then washed, drained and left to sprout in a warm place, until the shoots are about 6 mm (¼ in) long. This can take two to four days, according to the temperature.

The most universally popular seeds are the four varieties of millet seed: white, panicum, Japanese and red millet. These are usually mixed together. Plain canary seed is the next most frequently used with other seeds fed as required. Maw seed, rape, linseed and hemp seed (if available) and the black niger seed are useful, particularly during cold weather when body fat needs to be maintained. Hulled oats, groats and sunflower seed are usually fed to larger species. Parrotlike birds need adequate supplies of sunflower seeds and many eat maize and peanuts too.

A simple extra is clear honey which may be mixed with water in drinkers or even with seed for birds with young in the nest. Raw egg yolk may also be mixed with seed. Stale wholemeal bread, which has been well soaked, should be crumbled into small pieces and may have a little milk poured over it to form an ideal rearing aid. Any leftovers must be removed quickly lest the milk turn sour. Alternatively, the bread can be soaked in water, which is better if the remains cannot be removed promptly. Never use fresh bread for this purpose; it is too heavy to digest and can prove fatal to young birds.

Ample supplies of grit and cuttlefish bone are essential. Grit comes in several forms including oystershell, crushed granite and slate. Proprietary tonic grit in packet form may be purchased at pet food stores. It contains several vital minerals including salt, iron oxide, calcium, lime, phosphorus and a little charcoal. This preparation helps birds to masticate seed in the crop and therefore to digest their food properly. The calcium in cuttlefish bone is very high. Cuttlefish bone may be given both whole or flaked into small thin slivers.

Chicken egg shells are a very worthwhile source of added calcium, particularly important during the breeding season to help form healthy egg shells. Clean egg shell should be baked in the oven until very brittle and crushed into fine particles before feeding.

Charcoal is relished by certain seed-eaters, especially Australian finches. All types of grit should be provided in a separate dish to discourage birds from taking only their favourite kind from a selection.

If practical, annual or perennial seeding grass should be grown in the aviary. With these semi-ripe seeds available many types of birds successfully rear broods with little more than a hard seed diet.

Fresh greenfood should be fed on a regular basis as sporadic feeding can cause stomach upsets. New stock should be introduced to greenfood gradually and quantities increased as they become accustomed to it. Take care that any greenstuff has been obtained from areas free from insecticide spray, and that the food is always washed carefully. Chickweed (*Stellaria media*) is an important source of Vitamin E. Lettuce, dandelion and spinach are all useful. Among suitable seeding weeds are plantain (*Plantago lanceolata*), groundsel (*Senecio vulgaris*), shepherd's purse (*Capsella bursa pastoris*) and clover (*Trifolium pratense*). Thistles, such as *Carduus* and *Cirsium*, are enjoyed by many birds including the goldfinch. Frozen greenfood should never be given, as it chills the stomach. Some birds use left-over greenstuff in their nests during the breeding season and this damp material often helps in softening the egg shells, allowing the chicks to hatch easily.

Cod liver oil is a highly beneficial addition to the seed during cold weather and particularly in the breeding season to help prevent egg binding in young hens. Add 5 ml (1 teaspoon) of stabilised cod liver oil to ½ kg (2 lb 3 oz) of mixed millet, shake well and allow to stand for 24 hours before feeding to birds. Any uneaten oiled seed should be removed after a further 24 hours to prevent it from becoming rancid. This seed can then be washed and allowed to sprout before feeding so that it is not wasted. Oiled seed should be fed about once a month during summer and weekly in winter.

A liquid multi-vitamin preparation may be added to the birds' drinkers. Two drops are sufficient in a standard 50-cc (1 pint) drinker every other day.

During the breeding season breeding pairs may be supplied with proprietary brand canary rearing food mixed with

Right: *a Turquoisine Grass Parrakeet*
Below: *a Superb Spreo Starling*

Right: *a Yellow-Collared Ixulus*

finely mashed hard-boiled egg. This is a nourishing food for regurgitation by the parents for feeding to their young. It is best to start the parents on this before the young arrive, so they become accustomed to the mixture, and to check that they are feeding well. It should be given in the morning and uneaten mixture thrown away by dusk, or earlier in very warm regions, to ensure it is not tainted.

Ground birds, such as quail and small doves, require a seed mixture comprising equal parts of canary seed, mixed millets and a small quantity of hemp (if available) and groats. Wheat should be added to the diet of larger quail. Since quail are avid consumers of insectivorous food, meal worms, beetles and fresh ants' eggs should be offered.

For parrotlike species, add sunflower seed, fresh peanuts, groats and a small amount of hemp (if available) to mixed

Striped sunflower seed should be plump and hard

millets and plain canary seed. Sunflower and peanuts should make up about half of the mixture.

Large parrakeets enjoy other seeds such as buckwheat, whole oats, barley, wheat and maize. They enjoy small sweet apples, grapes, pears and bananas. All should be unbruised fruit of sound quality. They also like raw carrot and fresh sweetcorn (maize). They may also be given twigs to chew. Many types of wood are suitable, except laurel and laburnum, which are poisonous. Boiled sweetcorn (maize), should be fed in a separate dish, or its moisture makes seed turn mouldy.

Some birds prefer fruit containing seeds or pips and waste the flesh to reach them. Pomegranates are often enjoyed. Sponge cake soaked in a honey mixture may also be offered.

Parrotlike birds often suffer from a deficiency of Vitamin A in seed diets, so it is wise to provide a nectar mixture to rectify this. Two teaspoons of honey and two of rose hip syrup should be dissolved in water. If desired, add a few drops of a multi-vitamin preparation and perhaps alternate this with a meat extract. This provides ample quantities of Vitamins A and D. Other alternatives, such as malt, condensed milk and honey, may also be offered mixed with water. This should be given in dishes.

Most parrotlike birds love picking over a clod of earth with roots and grass attached. The trace elements manganese, iron, copper and zinc are often lacking in their diet and are provided in this way.

It is recommended that cooled, boiled water is always given to small seedeaters, particularly Australian species, such as Gouldians, who seem to thrive better on this. It is difficult to prevent birds drinking from other sources when they are kept outside, but at least the water in their drinkers should be boiled.

Australia and the State of California have declared the sale of hemp seed illegal. Sunflower seed provides the same nutrients as hemp.

DIET FOR SOFTBILLED BIRDS

The most important point to remember when feeding softbills is that careful attention should be paid to hygiene. Most of their food is perishable and should be freshly prepared at all times and any left-overs removed before they become tainted.

All softbills require more complicated feeding routines than seedeaters. The diet normally includes the following items.

Proprietary brands of both fine grade and coarse grade insectile mixtures for softbills can be obtained at pet food stores. The mixture should form a basic part of the diet, fine grade for the smaller species, including small insectivorous, omnivorous and frugivorous birds, and coarse grade for larger softbills, such as fruitsuckers, jays and starlings. Insectile mixtures are not perishable, but should be stored in airtight containers to preserve their moisture. These mixtures contain a well-balanced blend of proteins, carbohydrates, vitamins and minerals.

Nectar mixture is important to all types of softbills and essential for the nectivorous species. Proprietary brands of nectar powder may be purchased. These mixtures are easy to prepare in the correct strength. They may be mixed with pure clear honey and warm water, instead of sugar, if desired. Honey contains less carbohydrate than sugar, so provides less energy but is not so fattening. A very

active bird needs sugar, while a more lethargic species lives well on honey.

As many different types of fruit as possible should be offered. It must be ripe, but not over ripe, and unbruised. Chop all fruit into small cubes. Oranges, however, may sometimes be cut in half and suspended on pieces of string near a favourite perching spot.

Dried fruit, such as sultanas, currants and raisins, are rich in food value. They should be soaked for a few hours before feeding, and can be rather fattening. Bananas are enjoyed by birds but, again, can be fattening if fed too often. Do not feed any one fruit in excess. Cubed pieces of pear, apple, grape and melon may be given, plus berries, such as blackberries, raspberries and loganberries, cut in half.

Insects are very important for the insectivorous species and almost as necessary for other types too. Maggots should be cleaned thoroughly. Place them in an open container filled with bran. In two or three days they will have cleaned themselves thoroughly and the bran should be changed before they pupate into their first chrysalis. The maggots may be fed at any stage of their development cycle. In cool temperatures, the life cycle of the maggot slows down, but they should not be put under refrigeration, which stops them cleaning themselves. Mealworms should also be stored in bran which they eat. A culture may be set up quite easily or they may be purchased from pet food stores for convenience. They can also be fed to the birds during any stage of their life cycle. Make sure that the bran container has plenty of air by placing mesh over the top.

Locusts and crickets are another valuable food that may be purchased quite easily. The medium and larger softbills really enjoy these. Raw, minced meat, including beef, chicken and lamb, should be provided for the larger types. Do not let the meat go bad before being cleared away.

Hard-boiled egg, mashed or finely chopped, is useful. Although not easily digested, it is very nutritious. Cheese may be given, cut into small cubes. It is useful in winter, helping birds to put on an extra layer of fat, but should be fed more sparingly in warm weather.

Stale bread crumbled into small pieces and soaked in milk is much appreciated. As with seedeaters, never use fresh bread as it is too indigestible.

The propagation of fruit fly larvae is acceptable in certain countries, but prohibited in others. If allowed, it is quite easy to breed these in a barrel of rotten fruit which should be kept at a warm temperature. This can be done in a garden shed. Fruit flies are useful for small species. In Australia, termites known as white ants are a most valuable source of food for softbills.

Commercially prepared mynah bird pellets are available at pet food stores. These are fed dry. Even species as small as Pekin Robins eat and enjoy these. Many birds often prefer these to fruit and raw meat. The pellets contain several kinds of dried fruit, providing minerals and trace elements for improved plumage. They also have a high protein content, lack heavy oils and are easy to digest.

Peanut butter is another useful extra, although it may take some birds a little time to accept this addition. It is very nourishing and the easily digested oils are very good for plumage.

All dishes and drinkers should be washed in boiling water each day. Once a bird has accepted a well-balanced diet, it should not be changed or altered at random. Each fancier learns the particular preferences of his birds and it is wise to keep to a well-established routine.

OMNIVOROUS SOFTBILLS
This group includes MYNAHS, STARLINGS and JAYS.

Mixed fruit should account for almost half the daily ration, together with approximately 10% raw minced meat and 30% coarse-grade insectile mix. They should also be given soaked bread or sponge cake daily and around 10% livefood. All these ingredients should be mixed together in one dish. Occasionally they may be given hard-boiled egg as an additive. They should be offered plenty of plain boiled water.

Also included in the omnivorous group are BULBULS, FAIRY BLUEBIRDS, FRUITSUCKERS and the many different species of TANAGERS.

These birds need about 25% more fruit than the above group. Coarse-grade insectile mixture should make up about 10% of their diet. Raw minced meat and soaked sponge cake or soaked bread should be given in the same amounts but only around 5% livefood is necessary. Again all the items are to be mixed in the same dish. A dish of nectar is much appreciated and pure boiled water must always be provided.

FRUGIVOROUS SOFTBILLS
This group includes CEDAR WAXWINGS.

This group needs a large and varied amount of fruit. Coarse-grade insectile mix should be sprinkled over the fruit, encouraging the birds to eat this valuable item. About 10% raw minced meat should be given. Nectar powder may also be dusted over their fruit once a week or so, to add proteins, vitamins and minerals. The fruit itself is not sufficient to provide all the birds require. Boiled cubed potatoes, carrots and swedes may be added for a little more variety and extra vitamins and carbohydrates may also be given.

NECTIVOROUS SOFTBILLS

This group includes SUGARBIRDS, IXULUS and YUHINAS.

The mainstay of the diet is nectar, forming about 60% of their food. Fruit is a very important ingredient and should make up a further 25%. Soaked bread or sponge cake may be added and they need about 5% raw minced meat. Drinkers should always be scrupulously clean so that the nectar is not tainted. The fruit, meat and sponge cake or soaked bread should all be mixed together in one dish. In a separate dish, the birds should be given some fine-grade insectile mixture to which a few mealworms or maggots may be added. The insects should be coated in thick nectar, so that the insectile mix sticks to them. Avoid covering the heads, or they may die before being eaten. Fruit flies and an occasional spider are also enjoyed by these birds. Provide drinkers filled with plain boiled water.

INSECTIVOROUS SOFTBILLS

This group includes INDIAN BLUE ROLLERS.

Coarse-grade insectile mixture should be given to make up just under half the daily provision, plus about 15% mashed or chopped hard-boiled egg, maggots around 20% and mealworms a further 15%. Add a little cheese, either cubed or grated, and the same amount of grated carrot, plus some small chunks of raw meat. Mix all ingredients together, sprinkling the egg, maggots and mealworms on top. To help tame these birds, insects may be offered by hand at times. It is a good idea to try to collect smooth caterpillars, crickets, blowflies and spiders for feeding to birds. Some insectivorous species spurn mealworms and maggots since their normal prey moves faster, but try coating each maggot or mealworm with thick honey and some insectile mix. The heads must be left dry and uncoated.

CARNIVOROUS SOFTBILLS

This group includes HORNBILLS.

The main requirement is raw meat in cubes, heavily coated with coarse-grade insectile mixture. Half of the diet should be made up with dead, day-old chicks which may be purchased from pet food stores, and the occasional dead mouse. Nectar powder should be dusted on their foodstuff. Large locusts may be fed as a treat. In many ways their diet is similar to that of birds of prey. They also consume standard softbill fare, including fruit, soaked bread or sponge cake and cheese.

3
BREEDING

S uccessful breeding is achieved in six stages:

1 Courtship and display The cock bird performs a ritual to attract his desired mate. He may show off his colourful plumage, dance around his hen, or sing. Once a hen responds and accepts a partner, mating takes place.

2 Nest site selection followed by nest construction and preparation Nest sites are chosen with care and both birds usually carry materials in their beaks and sometimes tucked under their wings to the site. The nest is lined with moss, feathers (often plucked from their breasts) and other soft material.

3 Egg laying and incubation Once the hen begins to lay, the cock often feeds her, often on alternate days. He also stands guard at the entrance to the nest. One or both parents incubate their eggs.

4 Chicks hatch and feeding and rearing commence The young chicks are fed on regurgitated food supplied by their parents. Soft rearing food which is easily digested by the parents is of great help. Many birds also require insects to feed their young.

5 Chicks fledge and leave the nest Once the chicks have grown a covering of feathers comprised of down and an outer covering of quills, they are ready to emerge from the nest for the first time.

They usually return to the nest each night to roost. At this stage they are in juvenile plumage. The parents may still feed them, although they are now largely capable of feeding themselves.

6 Juvenile moult when youngsters become independent Young birds first moult when they are around three to four months old. They attain adult plumage and should now be able to fend for themselves. They should be closely observed to ensure that they are fit and healthy. This first moult is quite a strain on the body of young birds and they can be lost suddenly and unexpectedly. This is particularly true of the Gouldian Finch.

There are certain basic preparations that encourage birds to attempt to breed. A wide choice of nest boxes, baskets and other suitable receptacles should be made available. These facilities need to be well spaced out all over the accommodation at different levels. Plenty of cover encourages the birds to investigate these potential nesting sites. Nesting materials may be placed in the aviary, such as grasses, hemp teasings, fine wool, mosses, small twigs and chicken feathers.

Many birds are stimulated into breeding condition by the amount of daylight available, while others may attempt to breed at any time of the year. Most birds choose spring as their breeding season. You can help birds into peak condition by feeding soaked and sprouted seeds or extra livefood as the breeding season approaches. Oats are a useful aid as they stimulate birds into breeding condition. Remove the oats once the hen has commenced sitting, or the cock bird may pester his hen with continuing advances.

Do make sure that the birds are protected from heavy rainfall and that nest sites are not too exposed, particularly to harsh winds. Some nest boxes and baskets should be hung in the shelter, as many birds prefer this additional security. Nest boxes and baskets should not be moved around once they have been positioned as this only confuses the birds. No tidying up or cleaning of the flight should be contemplated at this time. The birds must feel secure and be disturbed as little as possible.

Once incubation commences, keep any inspection of the nests to the absolute minimum. Some birds will desert their nests at intrusion. If uncertain, leave well alone.

One of the problems most often encountered is that of chicks dying in the eggs before hatching, known as 'dead-in-shell'. This can be caused by a variety of factors: lack of humidity, dietary deficiencies or sometimes because the chick is unable to pierce the shell when it is time to hatch. Infertile eggs also account for a great many failures, particularly with young, inexperienced birds.

It is possible to determine whether eggs are fertile by holding them up to a strong light. An infertile or 'clear' egg will be very light in weight, lack colour definition and actually appear hollow. A well-filled egg is easily recognised.

Some parent birds throw their young out of the nest the minute they hatch, cock birds being the usual offenders. This is also attributed to inexperience in most cases.

Many large species, such as parrakeets, cockatiels and budgerigars, can be hand reared if necessary. An incubator or hospital cage is required. Hand rearing, although a time-consuming and tiring task, may be accomplished by those with patience. A temperature of 33°C (91°F) must be maintained for the chicks. A cardboard box, placed in a hospital cage, provides suitable housing. Paper tissues should be placed in the base of the box to absorb excrement.

The rearing mix should be made from milk and baby cereal in a thick consistency. An eye dropper (or a syringe) may be used for feeding small chicks. Larger

A ten-day-old Diamond Dove chick

A nest site with plenty of cover encourages breeding

A group of elegant and beautifully constructed weaver nests

chicks may be fed with a teaspoon. The sides of the teaspoon should be bent upwards to facilitate easy swallowing of food. As chicks develop, the mixture should be gradually thickened. It is helpful to add finely grated cuttlefish bone and fine powdered bonemeal to the mix to help form strong, healthy bones and claws.

Great care must be taken to avoid overloading the crop. It is easy to do this when using a syringe and a greedy bird often takes too much nourishment. When the crop appears overly distended, gentle massage often helps. All hand rearing tools should be warmed before use or chicks refuse to feed. Weaning should be accomplished by feeding soaked seed and soft fruits in most cases, using other foods for certain species.

Australian finches are not difficult birds to breed, however there may be one or two problems. If a young pair shows no interest in building a nest, it may be that either the cock or the hen is not yet in breeding condition or that the pair is incompatible. Sometimes it helps to separate the pair for a few weeks and then re-introduce them to one another, possibly offering them a further selection of nest boxes or baskets. Existing sites should not be removed. If, however, there is still no activity, consider changing their partners.

If the hens lay eggs but fail to incubate, this usually indicates a feeling of insecurity. It may help to adjust the boxes slightly to admit more light to the entrance. Gouldian cock birds, in particular, often refuse to enter a dark hole. Alternatively, a little more cover may be needed around the site. Most changes, however, should be kept to an absolute minimum. In many cases where parents are young and inexperienced, chicks may hatch and their parents may feed them insufficiently or not at all.

Masked Grassfinches and other Australian finches consume large quantities of charcoal when breeding and this should always be provided. They spend a lot of time on the ground and must not be allowed to become chilled. If they roost with damp feathers prior to egg hatching, this dampness can help to soften the egg shells for the young chicks to break out. But at other times it is not helpful since the parents can develop a cold.

Softbill breeding is easier to accomplish in a well planted aviary. Not only do these types require plenty of cover, but a good mixture of plants helps to encourage insects to inhabit the flight.

Many softbill species become pugnacious during the breeding season. Birds should be watched to make sure fighting does not take place and offenders may have to be segregated to their own quarters. Do not make it necessary for softbill pairs to compete for livefood by keeping too many birds together.

It may be worth while putting a compost heap in the aviary to provide a valuable source of small insects. Perhaps the easiest softbills to breed are the starling family, since their young will take maggots and small mealworms from a very early age.

Softbill chicks may also be hand reared in a hospital cage with a small pot of water, covered with a piece of mesh, for humidity. Very young chicks need feeding every hour from around 5 am in the morning to midnight, a somewhat daunting task. A week-old, medium sized softbill chick will require feeding every 90 minutes and a slightly older chick, every two hours. During winter months it is

A Bengalese chick, just hatched, among a clutch of eggs

necessary to provide twelve hours of light per day so that parents may feed their chicks properly.

Most parrotlike birds are hole nesters and logs and boxes are their chosen nesting sites. They should also be supplied with bark and rotting wood. They

A clutch of Budgerigar eggs

Three-day-old Budgerigar chicks

Above: *at six days old*

Above: *at eight days old*
Right: *at eleven days old*

appreciate plenty of humidity and in very warm weather their nesting sites should be sprayed with a fine mist to help eggs hatch satisfactorily. This is best done from outside the aviary if possible.

All breeding brids need extra food when there are more mouths to feed. As much soft food as possible should be given at this time. Parrotlike birds eagerly devour sweetcorn (maize) when rearing chicks. Many types of soft food may be given. Oatmeal porridge in medium consistency can be fed with crushed sunflower seeds (kernels only). Make sure, however, that the parents receive plenty of roughage. Greenfood and mashed carrot will be very welcome, but do not overfeed. Wholemeal bread in small quantities, moistened with honey and water, is another popular standby. Try to vary the diet as much as possible and note which foods are taken with the greatest eagerness.

Crushed rusks, stale white or wholemeal bread, soaked in milk and fortified with mashed hard-boiled egg, are very good for rearing chicks.

During the breeding season, extra care should be taken to make certain that all feeding dishes and drinkers are completely clean. Scald all dishes and tubes in boiling water daily. Remove uneaten food before it spoils. Prepare all feed in clean conditions and always wash your hands before preparation, particularly if you have been using household sprays, insecticides or perfumed substances of any kind.

Once birds have reared a maximum of two or three broods in a season, it is wise to segregate cocks from hens to prevent overbreeding, which only weakens the stock, resulting in inferior young. Hens may be lost if they are allowed to breed too often. It is often difficult to replace a hen as there are fewer hens for sale than cocks. Many cock birds pine for a lost mate and refuse to accept a new substitute for some time, thus ruining a whole breeding programme. Many species like to use a nest box to roost in throughout the year, so segregating cocks and hens means that you can allow them to do this without having to worry about them going to nest. If preferred, remove nest boxes and baskets instead, and leave cocks and hens together, but the cocks may still indulge in mating activities and try to find other nesting places.

Do not allow birds to go to nest before they are at least eight months of age, or preferably a year old. Young hens can suffer from egg binding, when the bird is unable to expel the egg from the oviduct. It is painful, distressing and can kill the bird.

Split ringing birds for identification purposes is helpful, especially to record their age, as is a system of small indexed record cards detailing hatching dates and progress.

Many fanciers ring their chicks with closed metal rings. It is normally advisable to do this if hoping to exhibit birds in shows in current year bred classes, since this proves that they are owner bred and is often a condition of entry. This entails removing the chicks from the nest. It should be done as quickly and carefully as possible. The age at which chicks are ringed varies according to their rate of development. Gouldian Finches, for example, are usually ready between 10 and 12 days of age. Never try to ring a chick if the leg has grown too large. Rings for particular species are obtainable from specialist suppliers or cage bird societies. Rings should fit well but not be too tight.

A selection of closed metal rings

Holding the bird's leg gently, fold back the rear claw and slip the ring over the front claws. It may be eased on to the leg with a match stick which has been filed to a point. Only one leg is rung. Rings are coded with letters and numbers relating to the breeder's surname, registration number and the year.

Split plastic rings in various colours may also be used to identify birds for pairing up at a later stage. They are not acceptable for exhibiting purposes. These may be used at any age, since they fit on to any size of leg.

Young budgerigars are always in great demand with pet stores. The well-organised fancier can find a good outlet here for surplus stock.

The keynote for success in breeding birds is patience. Give your birds time to adjust to their home. Feed them adequately at regular times and let them know that their home is a safe, secure and comfortable place before you expect too much from them. If they do not attempt to breed during their first season, they may well go to nest immediately the next season commences. Modify their quarters as little as possible unless the birds seem to be restless and insecure and always observe stock well before contemplating any major change.

Certain species are far more ready to breed and appear more domesticated than others. Try to start with the easy-to-breed species, then use that knowledge to help you breed the less willing types.

FOSTERING WITH BENGALESE

Bengalese are sometimes used to rear the chicks of Australian finches to increase the number of youngsters reared in a season. Eggs can be removed from a pair of Australian finches and placed under Bengalese, who then rear the chicks as their own. The pair of Australian finches then go on to produce more eggs.

Frequently, Bengalese are also used as foster parents for rearing chicks of those Australian finches who reject or refuse to feed their young.

There are one or two simple measures which are of great help if Bengalese are used as foster parents. Always use the largest and strongest pair of Bengalese you can find. Colour is immaterial for this purpose, only their health and willingness to rear chicks are important. If possible, obtain a pair which have already proved themselves to be willing fosters.

It is vital that the Bengalese pair chosen

is prepared to feed the youngsters properly. Before using these foster parents, try them with the chosen rearing food. If one or both of the brids only eat dry seed, do not use them and exchange them for another pair. A dry seed diet is not sufficient to rear healthy chicks. Test them first with a clutch of their own Bengalese youngsters to find out how well they rear chicks.

The young Bengalese may be split ringed for identification purposes and kept for future use. However, they should not be used to rear until they are at least eight months of age.

When fostering it is easier to provide more controlled conditions indoors than in an outside aviary. Whether inside or out, a fairly constant temperature of 20°C (68°F) is necessary to prevent the foster parents going into a moult during the rearing period, which would make them lose interest in feeding the young. Arrange the nest box in such a way that daily inspection is easily managed. Bengalese do not resent this.

When ready to use the Bengalese, try to ensure that the fostered eggs or chicks coincide as closely as possible with the hatching of their own eggs. Their own incubation period is 14 days and chicks leave the nest after three weeks. They do not object, however, if the fledging time of the foster chicks is different from their own. They do not have a specific nesting season and may go to nest at any time.

When placing eggs under Bengalese, give no more than six at a time. As all the eggs hatch at the same time, chicks belonging to more than one pair of Australian finches cannot be told apart. Try to keep accurate records as to how many clutches of eggs have been taken from each pair of Australian finches.

Most Australian finches will lay again eight or nine days after the last egg of the previous clutch is laid. If the eggs are taken away as soon as the last egg is laid, four or five clutches can be taken without overstraining the birds. A maximum of five clutches should be adhered to since inferior chicks result if any more are allowed.

As soon as the fostered chicks hatch, feed only sprouted seed which has been well washed and scalded for a few seconds in boiling water. Scalding removes some of the natural vitamins from the seed so it is beneficial to add two or three drops of a multi-vitamin preparation to the birds' drinking water. Fresh rearing food with mashed hard-boiled egg should be offered daily. Always stick to the same proprietary brand, in case the Bengalese are reluctant to eat a new type once rearing has started.

As soon as the last chick leaves the nest, remove the nest box. This stops the Bengalese laying again before the young Australian finches can feed themselves properly. Do not replace the nest box until after the young finches have been removed.

Sometimes Bengalese prefer wicker baskets to nest boxes and it is a good idea to try them with both.

Australian finches may be reared in greater numbers by using Bengalese as foster parents, but it is generally considered that parent-reared chicks are stronger than their fostered counterparts.

In a mixed collection, it should be pointed out that Bengalese can make a nuisance of themselves by trying to assist birds who do not require their help. It may be necessary to house them apart from other breeding birds at times, keeping them in reserve for emergencies.

4
AILMENTS

C areful management and feeding of birds ensure that illness is kept to a minimum, but there will be occasions when sickness is unavoidable. While some maladies are fairly simple to recognise and treat, there are many that are not. **When in doubt, consult your local veterinary surgeon.**

At the first sign of illness, isolate the bird from its companions. Signs of illness may include the bird sitting with its feathers puffed up and generally looking out of sorts, very loose droppings, and often watery or half closed eyes.

The best treatment available for a sick bird is the prompt provision of heat. Reliable hospital cages may be purchased. Most birds possess a body temperature of 40°C (104°F). As soon as a bird becomes ill, its body temperature drops drastically and this must be avoided at all costs.

The hospital cage should be set at 24°C (76°F). Normally a mild antibiotic also helps, but care should be taken with any medicine since overdosing can prove fatal. Adequate food supplies and favoured tit-bits should be placed in the hospital cage to encourage the sick bird to eat. Plenty of boiled drinking water should be made available.

Reduce the temperature gradually when the bird shows active signs of recovery. The light in the hospital cage should be left on 24 hours a day to allow the bird to feed whenever it desires. Once the bird is eating well again, it is a sure sign that it is recovering, but it should not be allowed to rejoin the aviary until it is back to its normal self.

When using your hospital cage make sure the perches are placed close to the floor or removed entirely if the sick bird is not strong enough to perch. When the bird is able to grip again, they may be replaced. The bird's ability to perch properly again is another sign of improvement.

ABSCESS Parrotlike species often develop abscesses around the cere or beak area. These may be confused with tumours. They must only be removed by a veterinary surgeon and an antibiotic applied to prevent reinfection. They can be caused by bacterial agents.

ASPERGILLOSIS This condition results from a lack of hygiene and is caused by the bird inhaling an airborne fungus called *Aspergillus fumigatus*. It occurs mostly in the larger kinds of parrotlike bird, but it can affect small parrakeets, although not usually budgerigars. Difficulty in breathing may be accompanied by a discharge from the bird's nostrils. Some fanciers add potassium iodine to their birds' drinking water (2½ grains to 4 tablespoons of water) as a preventative.

ASTHMA The symptoms are wheezing and heavy, laboured breathing. Symptoms may develop following a cold. Other causes of asthma include infection of the lungs and air sacs, aspergillosis (see above) and the inhalation of pollen or poisonous fumes. This condition may take several months to eradicate. A bird with asthma will usually be seen to have a gaping beak and ruffled feathers. The bird's sinus passages often become clogged and treatment should consist of a decongestant cold remedy and a medium strength inhalant administered every day. These remedies may be purchased in the correct strength for birds from pet stores or supplied by a veterinary surgeon. Electric vaporizers may be used to ease the application of the inhalant. Parrakeets and budgerigars are the most likely types to suffer from this complaint.

BACTERIAL INFECTION Symptoms are diarrhoea, loss of appetite and listlessness. Prevention is good hygiene and a regular, thorough cleaning of the aviary with disinfectant. A new bird should be kept in isolation for a period of 30 days, before being placed in the aviary, to make sure it is not carrying any unpleasant virus.

BLEEDING This must be stopped promptly with the use of a blood coagulant, such as hydrogen peroxide, applied with damp cotton wool.

BROKEN BONES A broken wing is often the result of a night fright when a bird flies into something in the dark. A broken leg can be the result of a bird catching a leg in aviary netting. Most birds recover from these fairly easily on their own without any treatment. Broken wings, however, sometimes result in a permanent deformity which may affect a bird's flying ability. The bird should be placed in a hospital cage with its perch near the floor. The enforced idleness prevents the bird from using the affected part. Slings and splints are not always effective, but if desired, a splint can be made from lollipop sticks or feather quills.

BUMBLEFOOT Finches and softbills sometimes suffer from this painful condition, particularly in old age. The feet become swollen and lumpy deposits resembling cheese appear on them. Since the treatment involves making small incisions in these substances and gently squeezing out the mass, it should be done extremely carefully. A blood coagulant should also be applied. It is advisable to have this done by a veterinary surgeon, as it is very painful for the bird. Shock or heart failure could result if it is not done properly.

CANCER Cancers in birds appear as lumps and may be visible or internal. While some external types may be removed, others are not treatable. In these cases it may be kinder to have the sufferer put painlessly to sleep.

CATARACTS Scales forming across the eye may be caused by poor diet over a prolonged period of time. Little can be done for this condition.

COCCIDIOSIS An uncommon disease caused by a microscopic organism called *Coccidia*. It affects the intestines. The bird becomes weak and emaciated and may have bloody diarrhoea. Sulphur drugs may be added to the drinking water, but it is difficult to cure and spreads alarmingly rapidly. It should not occur if good hygiene is practised; particular care is needed in hot weather.

COLDS Place the bird in a hospital cage at the first sign of a cold. The temperature should be set at 25°C (80°F). A bird with a cold sits with its feathers puffed out, in a hunched position. The eyes may water and appear to be half closed. If severe catarrh is present, the bird opens and closes its beak frequently. Lack of appetite usually accompanies a cold. A mild cold remedy may be obtained from your pet store and an inhalant is also useful. A few vitamin drops and a little honey may be added to the drinking water.

CONJUNCTIVITIS A painful eye inflammation caused by a virus, fungi, bacteria or some other irritant. An affected bird rubs its eye on a perch, blinks a great deal and there may be a watery or yellowish discharge from the eye. Prompt treatment by a veterinary surgeon with an antibiotic should help.

CONSTIPATION The bird will be seen to be straining and any droppings passed may be small, dry and hard. Greenfood and Vitamin B added to the drinking water help. Two tablespoons of black strap molasses mixed into a quart of distilled water and given to the bird to drink also helps.

CROP IMPACTION The crop can become blocked by food or as a result of a digestive disorder. A swelling appears on the lower neck and the bird appears to be trying to vomit. Surgery is usually necessary.

CYSTS Yellow skin cysts, or non-malignant growths, often on the wings, are very common in budgerigars. They are easily removed by a veterinary surgeon.

DEAD-IN-SHELL Many different factors may account for the chicks of breeding birds being found dead in their shells. One or both parents may be immature or too old. It may be caused by a genetic factor or dietary deficiency in certain vitamins and minerals, such as B and E group vitamins. Toxic substances may be responsible, such as DDT ingested by the parents at some time. The egg shell may be too thick or the chick stuck to the inner membrane. There may be a failure by the parents to incubate the egg properly or a lack of humidity. Try to establish the cause.

DIARRHOEA This condition is usually a symptom of other illness and is rarely caused by a diet problem. Two tablespoons of black strap molasses in a quart of distilled water may be given to the bird to drink. If no improvement is noticed within a few days, consult your veterinary surgeon.

EGG BINDING A very common problem, occurring frequently in young hens, and occasionally in mature hens. The bird is seen to be straining as though constipated. She is unable to expel the egg and once her strength is exhausted, death may quickly follow. The vent is puffy and swollen and the egg can be felt by touching around the area very gently with the forefinger. No pressure should be applied. Gentle bathing with warm water around the vent and a little warmth may help. This condition may be prevented by mixing a little cod liver oil with seed mixture for hardbills. Cold weather can also cause this problem, so young hens should not be allowed to breed in particularly cold weather. Prevent the associated condition of soft shelled eggs by providing plenty of cuttlefish bone and grits. Inadequate diet, lack of calcium and exercise often give rise to both these conditions in mature hens. Always provide a mineral supplement for breeding birds.

EGG SAC RUPTURE Rupture is caused when the hen expels not only the egg, but the egg sac membrane or oviduct as well. The egg must be gently forced through the opening and the membrane eased back into the vent, with a finger moistened with a saline solution to prevent infection of the delicate tissues.

ENTERITIS Symptoms are inflammation of the small intestine normally accompanied by diarrhoea. Droppings are watery and often green. The bird seems to drink a great deal and eat large quantities of grit. The vent is messy and the bird can be seen to be straining. Infectious enteritis is very dangerous and can destroy a whole aviary if the affected bird is not isolated at once. Overcrowding and dirty conditions are the usual cause. New imports that have not been properly acclimatised may bring this infection with them, so never add a new bird to your stock without keeping it separate for as long as 30 days. If enteritis is present, it is usually evident within a week. The bird must be placed in a hospital cage and given a medication containing sulfa methazine. The hospital cage must be disinfected after use.

FEATHER MITE AND QUILL MITE Suspect mites when a bird's wings and tail look as though they have been chewed. A mild, gentle insecticide spray, specifically designed for birds, should eradicate the mites.

FEATHER PLUCKING Most feather plucking is performed by birds on their neighbours, although a bird suffering from boredom or desire for a mate often plucks itself. Some people feel a dietary deficiency may account for this tendency. Sometimes a bully in the collection plucks the feathers of a weaker bird and may eventually make an attack to kill. Bullies should be removed and placed with larger birds.

FITS Mynah birds are often subject to fits caused by improper diet and lack of exercise. Overexposure to the sun can also cause fits in other species of tropical birds.

FRENCH MOULT If young birds, particularly budgerigars, show abnormal feather moult, which persists even when they are mature, this condition is known as French moult. Wing and tail feathers continually moult. Overbreeding, incorrect feeding and perhaps an inherited factor are said to be the causes. It is better not to breed from such birds.

GOING LIGHT The term 'going light' is applied to a sickly-looking bird that loses weight rapidly. It is a symptom which may indicate a variety of other conditions. In extreme cases, it may mean tuberculosis. Loss of appetite causes weight loss very rapidly. Death may result, so birds seen to exhibit this tendency should be isolated in a hospital cage and encouraged to start eating again as soon as possible. In some cases nothing seems to help and the bird dies. It is advisable to obtain a post mortem when this occurs in case another bird should suffer this condition.

GOITRE Goitre shows as a swelling on the neck. Only budgerigars, and usually only hens, suffer from this affliction. Incorrect functioning of the thyroid gland is the cause and can be brought on by breeding. Treatment with iodine blocks is the usual remedy. An affected hen must not breed.

GOUT The legs, wings and neck are affected with a deposit of a hard white substance around the joints. It occurs rarely, and mainly in budgerigars and parrots, usually following a kidney infection. Massage under an anaesthetic is the normal treatment.

HEART DISEASE Heart attacks usually prove fatal and occur mainly in older birds or birds that have a sudden shock or fright. Mild cases of heart disease may sometimes be helped by treatment with drugs.

LICE Lice sometimes appear on birds. Affected birds are restless, unable to settle, and scratch and rub their skin. Pyrethrum powder is a very safe and effective treatment.

LIMBERNECK OR BOTULISM Botulism is a deadly poison which gives rise to the condition known as 'limberneck', a form of paralysis that starts in the bird's neck and gradually affects the whole body. The organism is found in dirty water and rotten food that attracts flies. There is no cure.

MANGE MITE Budgerigars and large parrakeets are sometimes affected by these mites. They affect beaks, ceres and other facial areas.

MOULT Birds moult twice a year, in spring and autumn, each moult normally lasting about six weeks. Birds look very scruffy during this phase. A careful watch should be kept and any bird that appears to be out of condition should be isolated and kept warm. Extra dietary supplements may be given to finches at this time and standard canary moulting food is very useful. Softbills should be given liquid vitamins and minerals; the best supplements come in powder form and sprinkle easily over their normal dishes. Any moult occurring outside spring or autumn, known as the 'soft moult', may be the result of sun shining on a bird through glass, or of one bird being bullied by another.

NEPHRITIS Inflammation of the kidneys is known as nephritis. This disease is common in all types of birds. The bird becomes listless, sits with ruffled feathers and drinks a lot of water. Droppings are white.

ORNITHOSIS (psittacosis) Once a very dread disease since it was fatal if contracted by humans. Thankfully it is no longer deadly, although it still causes very unpleasant pneumonia-like symptoms in humans and can make one seriously ill. It is a virus disease that causes lethargy, green diarrhoea, breathing difficulties and a discharge from eyes and nostrils. It is treatable if caught in time. Recovery is slow. It is usually found only in newly imported birds.

OVERGROWN BEAK AND TOENAILS Certain species exhibit a tendency towards overgrown toenails which can catch in aviary netting. It is quite easy to trim overgrown nails with fingernail clippers, taking care not to cut into the vein. If a vein is nipped inadvertently, stop the bleeding with hydrogen peroxide. The beak, if overgrown, may also be trimmed.

PNEUMONIA An untreated cold may easily turn to pneumonia. Keep an affected bird warm. Swift treatment with aureomycin or sulfa methaxine is important.

PSITTACOSIS see ORNITHOSIS

RED MITE Red mites are most prevalent during hot summer weather. Living in corners and crevices by day, they emerge at night to feed on the blood of birds. They can reduce a bird to a very anaemic state and even kill it. Pyrethrin is the safest standard aerosol exterminator of this pest, slower in effect than some other brands, but very safe for birds. It does not contaminate their food or water. South American softbills, when newly imported, often carry with them some unusual lice and mites and should be well sprayed before being introduced to the aviary.

REGURGITATION Most birds regurgitate to feed their mates or young. Sometimes birds regurgitate to feed their favourite person as a sign of affection. Regurgitation for other reasons may denote illness, such as crop impaction, sour crop or mould. Simple indigestion or sometimes a cold, when the bird will regurgitate mucus, may cause this too.

RHEUMATISM A painful swelling of the joints, which often occurs in older birds. Very little can be done to alleviate it, although massage can sometimes help.

RICKETS This can occur in many birds, but particularly in young budgerigars. Incorrect diet, deficient in Vitamin D, causes the bird to have short, badly shaped legs with swollen joints. The bird is weak and unable to fly. Bone meal and Vitamin D3 should be added to the feed.

SALMONELLOSIS This is caused by *Salmonella* bacteria. It is often fatal to birds and can be transmitted to human beings. The symptoms include lethargy, diarrhoea, dysentery and excessive thirst. Convulsions normally occur followed by sudden death. If suspected, the bird's droppings should be analysed. Early treatment with the correct antiobiotics from a veterinary surgeon will normally cure it. The bird's quarters must then be thoroughly disinfected.

SCALY FACE AND SCALY LEG This condition is caused by a small mite. Yellowish-white crusts form on the beak, around the cere and eyes, and sometimes on the legs and around the vent. Treat with a 10% solution of benzyl benzoate applied with cotton wool every day for a week. Prompt treatment should be given, as severe cases can lead to deformity of the beak.

SHOCK Shock may be caused by a number of factors. Rough handling is the most frequent cause. Night frights, too, can cause shock and may lead to a heart attack.

SINUS DISORDER Sinus problems often appear after a cold. The bird has clogged nostrils and watering eyes. A badly impacted sinus often creates a large swollen nodule of hard mucus substance. The nodule must be lanced by pricking with a sterilised needle. A scab forms and is later easily removed by gentle massage. Gently work off all the hard mucus with damp cotton wool or a cotton bud to prevent recurrence of this condition.

SOFT-SHELLED EGGS This is often caused by a calcium deficiency. It seems to occur most often in budgerigars. Many fanciers use calcium boroglucanate administered directly or in drinking water to prevent this.

SORE FEET Birds sometimes get sore feet if seed husks and droppings get stuck to them. The resulting irritation causes little sores to form. The feet must be dipped in warm water mixed with mild disinfectant and the hard lumps gently washed off. Gently towel dry the feet and lightly apply some Vaseline, making sure it is absorbed. The bird should be treated several times if necessary.

SOUR CROP Sour crop is caused by a digestive upset and can result in a strong, unpleasant smell. A teaspoon of baking soda should be mixed into a quart of water and given to the bird over a period of two days.

SWOLLEN OIL GLAND The oil gland is located at the base of the tail and contains oil used in preening and grooming. Sometimes the oil clogs up the gland and a sore and inflamed swelling is caused. A toothpick, matchstick or damp cotton wool bud should be used to remove the offending material with very gentle pressure.

WORMS Worms occur more often in parrotlike species than in other birds. Cleanliness is the best method of prevention. Your veterinary surgeon will prescribe a proprietary brand worming product.

5
HOW TO SELECT COMPATIBLE BIRDS

B efore purchasing birds, it is a good idea to visit some bird gardens, zoos and private aviaries to look at their healthy specimens. Compare the different types and observe their behaviour closely.

The choice of dealer is most important when buying birds. Check up on as many different sources as possible, as pet stores vary tremendously in the quality and selection of birds on offer. Do try to take as much time as possible over this. It is often better to wait a little longer for the birds of your choice, rather than to buy inferior stock. It may also be possible to obtain birds from experienced fanciers who wish to sell their surplus stock.

There are some basic points to watch for when trying to select healthy birds:

1 Make sure the bird is not sitting huddled up with feathers puffed out.
2 Ensure that the eyes are clear and open, showing no signs of a watery discharge.
3 Check the vent to make sure it is clean and unsoiled. It should not appear to be damp.
4 Make sure that the legs and feet are undamaged and toe nails are intact.
5 Examine the nostrils to see that they are clear and free from discharge.
6 Feel the breast bone of larger birds to see that there is a fair amount of flesh on the breast.

Do not worry unduly about the appearance of the plumage. Moulting birds often look quite scruffy, as do those that are feather plucked or have had wings clipped by dealers or exporters. Feathers soon grow again and a bath often makes a bird look much better. The only point to remember when purchasing a moulting bird is that its general health may be a little under par and extra nourishment may be required (see feeding chapter, page 28).

When trying to choose a true pair of birds of a species where no sexual differences are visible or described, it is advisable to purchase several birds and allow them to pair up. This usually results in at least one true pair and the surplus may then be sold or exchanged.

When purchasing birds, note that very healthy specimens often sit balanced on one foot while perching or roosting. This is usually a good sign, although some healthy birds resolutely perch on both feet. A bird that is seen to be busily preening its feathers is generally a fit bird, interested in its appearance and in reasonable health. If a bird is at the feeding dish, look for signs of a healthy appetite. Avoid a bird that appears to be gorging itself on grit. Too much grit indicates a poor or sluggish digestion. In general, choose a bird which appears fairly lively and interested in its surroundings.

Keep new birds in separate cages in the bird room or shelter for a short period before releasing them into an outside aviary. Remember to acclimatise birds that are to live outside. They should not be transferred from an indoor site to an immediate drop in temperature, although this need not be a problem if the weather is warm or if the bird has come from another outside location.

When choosing birds it is important to select only those which can live together in harmony. Incompatible birds fight over favourite perching spots, nesting

COMPATIBILITY GROUPS

Group 1 ●	Group 2 ○	Group 3 ■
African Silverbill	Bengalese	African Silverbill
Bengalese	Bicheno	Bengalese
Bicheno	Chestnut-Breasted Finch	Bicheno
Chinese Painted Quail	Chinese Painted Quail	Canary
Cordon Bleu Waxbill	Cordon Bleu Waxbill	Chestnut-Breasted Finch
Golden-Breasted Waxbill	Diamond Dove	Chinese Painted Quail
Green Singing Finch	Diamond Sparrow	Diamond Dove
Green Twinspot	Gouldian Finch	Diamond Sparrow
Indian Zosterops	Green Singing Finch	Goldfinch
Lavender Finch	Green Twinspot	Gouldian Finch
Orange-Cheeked Waxbill	Long-Tailed/Heck's Grassfinch	Green Singing Finch
Peter's Twinspot	Masked Grassfinch	Green Twinspot
Red Avadavat	Peter's Twinspot	Long-Tailed/Heck's Grassfinch
Red-Eared Waxbill	Pin-Tailed Parrot Finch	Masked Grassfinch
Spice Bird	Pin-Tailed Whydah	Peter's Twinspot
Star Finch	Purple Glossy Starling	Pin-Tailed Parrot Finch
Vinaceous Fire Finch	Red Avadavat	Pin-Tailed Whydah
Violet-Eared Waxbill	Red-Billed Quelea	Purple Glossy Starling
Zebra Finch	Spice Bird	Spice Bird
	Star Finch	Star Finch
	Three-Coloured Mannikin	Three-Coloured Mannikin
	Vinaceous Fire Finch	White-Headed Mannikin
	Violet-Eared Waxbill	Zebra Finch
	White-Headed Mannikin	
	Zebra Finch	

sites and feeding dishes. Unhappy birds refuse to breed and, in extreme cases, severe injuries, such as damaged toes or the loss of an eye, can be caused, particularly amongst the parrotlike species.

The guide list shown below suggests eight 'compatibility' groups.

It must be emphasised that these groups are a guide only – always remember that there are individual birds who may have aggressive tendencies. Watch out for bullies and isolate individuals where necessary. It is often better to sell such a bird, rather than to wait and hope

COMPATIBILITY GROUPS

Group 4   □

Bourke's Parrakeet
Budgerigar
California Quail
Cockatiel
Elegant Grass Parrakeet
Laughing Dove
Plum-Headed Parrakeet
Red-Rumped Parrakeet
Splendid Grass Parrakeet
Turquoisine Parrakeet

Group 5   ◀

Budgerigar
California Quail
Cut-Throat Finch
Green Cardinal
Japanese Hawfinch
Java Sparrow
Laughing Dove
Magpie Mannikin
Napoleon Weaver
Pin-Tailed Whydah
Pope Cardinal
Red-Billed Quelea
Red-Crested Cardinal
Yellow Sparrow
Yellow-Backed Whydah

Group 6   ◇

Canary
Goldfinch
Green Cardinal
Japanese Hawfinch
Java Sparrow
Magpie Manikin
Napoleon Weaver
Pekin Robin
Pope Cardinal
Red-Billed Quelea
Red-Crested Cardinal
Yellow Sparrow
Yellow-Backed Whydah

Group 7   ◆

Andaman Mynah
Black-Chinned Yuhina
Black-Crested Bulbul
Blue-Capped Tanager
Cedar Waxwing
Emerald-Spotted Tanager
Indian Blue Roller
Indian Zosterops
Pagoda Mynah
Pekin Robin
Purple Sugarbird
Rothschild's Mynah
Yellow-Collared Ixulus
Yellow-Winged Sugarbird

Group 8   △

Andaman Mynah
Asian Fairy Bluebird
Cedar Waxwing
Golden-Fronted Fruitsucker
(a single bird only, pairs
are too aggressive)
Indian Blue Roller
Pagoda Mynah
Pileated Jay
Rothchild's Mynah
Superb Spreo Starling
(a single bird only, pairs
are too aggressive)
White-Crested Laughing
Thrush

it may change its ways. Sometimes, however, the addition of another dominant type may alter the situation.

It is a good idea for the novice bird keeper to start his collection with seed-eaters, possibly moving on to the more difficult softbill species at a later stage.

The most easily managed species of seedeaters are the Zebra Finch, Bengalese and many of the small waxbills. Australian Grassfinches, while relatively easy to care for, may need extra warmth. Budgerigars, cockatiels and small parrakeets, such as Bourke's Parrakeet, are very simple to care for.

Where parrotlike birds are concerned, very few species may be kept together. Only the species mentioned in Group 4 should be mixed, sparingly, in as much space as possible. Do not be tempted to try to house any of the lovebird species in a mixed collection. They may look small and beautiful, but their sharp, curved beaks can be lethal. They should only be kept in pairs in individual housing. The Fischer's Lovebird is the only species which may safely be kept in a colony of its own breed. Never put lovebirds in with finches for they will certainly attack.

The same warning applies to all the small species of parrot, such parrakeets as conures and all the nectar-feeding parrakeets.

The size of the aviary has a considerable influence on the success of mixing various species. Birds are always less tolerant of one another in a small enclosure than in a larger area, as they are territorial creatures who like to claim the largest spot for themselves.

Smaller birds are content with a smaller area for their own preserve than the larger species. Breeding pairs must be allotted more space than single specimens. If there is very little space available, consider keeping only single cock birds of individual species. In this way, it is possible to house a colourful collection of attractive birds without risk of fighting.

Some birds prefer densely planted aviaries, which provide the best cover for nest building and privacy for the more timid and shy birds. If keeping birds such as the Chinese Painted Quail and other ground species, take care not to tread on their eggs or young.

Providing several roosting spots, nesting sites and feeding dishes prevents arguments between birds. Too few roosting spots or nesting sites in the accommodation means fighting can break out even amongst the most placid birds. Nest boxes and baskets should be placed as far apart as possible and evenly distributed around the quarters.

When introducing new birds of any kind to a mixed collection, it is useful to provide an extra place for the new birds to feed, so that they do not interfere with the usual feeding routine.

It is quite easy to keep birds of similar size and habits together. If a smaller type is introduced to the collection it is likely to be bullied, likewise if a larger type is brought in it often tries to dominate the rest.

In their natural state, birds operate a 'pecking order': the stronger dominate and rule the weaker. This order is often observed in a captive collection and when a newcomer is introduced it is certainly noticed. Such encounters are best kept to a minimum and should be watched closely. In a few days the normal order should be restored. Large omnivorous birds and insect-eating species should only be kept together when they are of similar size, strength and habit.

6
A-Z OF SUITABLE SPECIES FOR A MIXED COLLECTION

E ach of the birds in this chapter is suitable for inclusion in a mixed collection. The 71 birds described fit into eight groups, as listed on page 52 and 53. The description of each bird carries a symbol or symbols relevant to its group or groups. Careful reference to these symbols prevents the fancier from mixing unsuitable types in an aviary.

AFRICAN SILVERBILL
Lonchura malabarica *(in colour*
cantans *page 95)*
Origin: West and Central Africa

An adaptable, easy-to-breed species which also incubates the eggs of other birds and rears their young, the African Silverbill has many other advantages. It is hardy and can withstand extremes of temperature. It lives happily with other small seedeaters.

There is also an Indian Silverbill (*Lonchura malabarica*) but this is not such a hardy bird.

Description:
Size: 10 to 12 cm (4 to 4½ in)
COCK:
Head: creamy-brown. Body: creamy-brown. Wings: dark brown. Underparts: pale buff. Rump: black. Tail: black. Beak: silver. Legs: dull pink.

HEN:
Alike, so it is impossible to sex these birds by appearance. It is best to purchase several birds and allow them to choose their own mate. The cock has a pleasant song.

Diet: (Seedeater)
Plain basic canary seed and mixed millets form the basic diet. Millet sprays are also relished and occasional greenfood, grit and cuttlefish bone should be provided.

Breeding:
The African Silverbill has a very peaceful nature and breeds happily among other species of small birds, such as waxbills, in a mixed collection. Several pairs often nest at the same time and may help each other in the feeding of their chicks, once they are all out on the perches.

This bird may sometimes develop the unfortunate habit of making 'sandwich nests'. The bird constructs a nest, lays eggs and then immediately makes another nest on top. To prevent this, nest boxes or baskets should be filled with nesting material, tightly packed with a small amount of space left for the birds to complete their preparations. A quiet place must be selected for the nest boxes and baskets. The birds use soft materials such as mosses, soft grasses and feathers, constructing a narrow slip-in entrance.

Four eggs form the normal clutch and

the incubation period is 12 days. While feeding the young, the parents should be given some extras such as soaked bread and hard-boiled egg, some chopped mealworms and fresh ants' eggs. Soaked and sprouted seed is better than dry seed during the breeding season.

This bird hybridises with the Spice Bird quite frequently and is prepared to hatch and rear the young of restless sitters, such as the Cordon Bleu and the Red-Eared Waxbill.

This species also interbreeds with Bengalese, so these can be used as foster parents in emergencies.

It is quite possible for one pair of African Silverbills to rear 20 young in one season. The group may all be left together to form a colony and true pairs may be identified with split plastic rings.

ANDAMAN MYNAH ◆ △
Sturnus erythropygius   *(in colour*
andamanensis   *page 90)*
Origin: Andaman and Nicobar Islands

The Andaman Mynah is a lively, inquisitive bird. A single bird or a pair can safely be kept in an aviary containing similar types, without aggression. The Andaman Mynah is easy to tame and can be taught to take mealworms from the hand. It is a good exhibition species.

Description:
Size: 20 cm (8 in)
COCK:
Head: white. Breast: white merging into light grey underneath. Back: light grey. Rump: white. Wings: black with a green sheen on outer flights. Tail: black tipped with white. Beak and legs: yellow. Eyes: white.

HEN:
Identical. Difficult to sex by appearance, so observe behaviour.

Diet: (Softbill)
Insectile mix, fruit and fresh ants' eggs form the basic diet. Occasional mealworms should be provided, but too many make this bird fat. This species sometimes picks up and eats a little millet seed.

The Andaman Mynah likes to bathe, so a pool in the aviary is welcomed, and it chatters and calls excitedly as it splashes around.

It can stand extremes of heat and cold, but needs protection from frosty conditions.

Breeding:
Few captive breedings have been recorded for this bird. Plenty of livefood must be provided, if breeding is to be encouraged. Mealworms and fresh ants' eggs should be mixed with soil and sand in a bowl. A piece of freshly dug turf is much enjoyed, turned over so it may be picked at. Plenty of cover and a selection of nest sites are needed.

(Pagoda Mynah, see page 105. Rothschild's Mynah, see page 123.)

ASIAN FAIRY BLUEBIRD △
Irene puella
Origin: India, Thailand and South East Asia

An easy-to-manage, fruit-biased omnivorous softbill, which, once acclimatised, is hardy enough to winter outside, needing only a frost-proof shelter. It has a melodious call and makes a very delightful sight flying in the aviary with its bright

An Asian Fairy Bluebird cock

COCK:
Mantle: blue. Back and area down to base of tail: blue. Other areas: shiny, velvet black. Eyes: red with black pupils.
HEN:
Very similar, but a far more dusky blue. Both cock and hen birds are heavy bodied.

Diet: (Softbill)
Bananas, pears, oranges, soft fruit, currants, sultanas and raisins form the basic diet. Raw minced meat should be given and honey and water mixture poured over sponge cake or stale bread makes a welcome addition to the diet. Livefood, such as mealworms and well-cleaned maggots, is necessary. Hard-boiled egg mash is enjoyed. All these ingredients can be mixed together in one dish in the following percentages: 65% fruit, 10% raw minced meat; 10% sponge cake or bread; 10% coarse grade insectile mix and 5% livefood. Nectar mix made from proprietary brand nectar powder and honey and water, or sugar and water, may be given in a dish on its own.

Breeding
The Asian Fairy Bluebird is not too difficult to persuade to breed. It is sometimes difficult to obtain pairs of this attractive species, but zoos and bird gardens occasionally part with surplus stock to keen fanciers.

Pairs use a shallow cup-shaped nesting basket if provided, lined with fine grasses and moss. If left to build their own, they make untidy looking nests in dense bushes, quite high up. Just two small olive grey eggs with brown speckles are laid. Plenty of livefood is necessary for chick rearing.

The Asian Fairy Bluebird is fairly

blue colour and engaging ways. It has very small, delicate feet in relation to its body size and its toes must be protected from frost bite.

This species is able to fly very strongly and needs a spacious aviary. If unable to obtain a pair, one sole cock bird lives quite happily on its own among similar types in a mixed collection, and becomes very tame.

Description:
Size: 25 cm (10 in)

docile in a mixed collection of birds of similar size. During the breeding season, however, cock birds can be bad tempered towards their own kind if several pairs are kept in the same aviary.

BENGALESE FINCH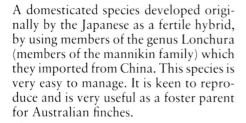
Lonchura domestica
Origin: China and Japan

A domesticated species developed originally by the Japanese as a fertile hybrid, by using members of the genus Lonchura (members of the mannikin family) which they imported from China. This species is very easy to manage. It is keen to reproduce and is very useful as a foster parent for Australian finches.

Description:
Size: 13 cm (5 in)
Several different colour forms exist including white, chocolate and white, chestnut and white, fawn and crested.
COCK:
Beak: Two-tone colour. Body: white with either chocolate, chestnut or fawn patterning. Markings vary greatly. Wings and tail usually show plenty of white. Legs: dark or pale.
HEN:
As cock. Both birds are stocky with a heavy beak.

The sex of Bengalese cannot be determined by physical appearance, only by behaviour. The cock bird puffs himself up to resemble a small balloon while singing. It is recommended that several

Fawn and White Bengalese Finches

true pairs of Bengalese are kept for fostering orphans in a mixed collection of finches.

Bengalese love to bathe and should be provided with suitable facilities. This species may need to have its nails clipped.

Diet: (Seedeater)
Plain canary seed and mixed millets form the basic diet. Millet sprays and sprouted seed may be given as a treat. Grit and cuttlefish bone must always be available.

Breeding:
Bengalese commence breeding as early as eight months of age. Nest boxes should be provided with a rather small entrance hole, much preferred by this species. A rather untidy nest is made inside the box and the birds like to be well hidden while incubating. Six to eight eggs are normally laid and both parents sit side by side in the nest during the incubation period of 14 days. The young are carefully fed by both parents for about 21 days. When rearing their young, Bengalese should be provided with egg food, soaked bread, mealworms and some greenfood. A few drops of cod liver oil may be added to the rearing food for young chicks. Youngsters should be given soaked seed for the early weeks of their life. Once independent, Bengalese may be kept on dry seed outside the breeding season.

BICHENO FINCH ● ○ ■
Stizoptera bicheonovii
Origin: Australia

The smallest Australian finch, suitable for a mixed collection of similar sized birds as it is good tempered and docile, although it defends its nest vigorously.

A Bicheno Finch

This is a lively, amusing bird. It is hardy and although it prefers a temperature of 15°C (60°F), it will survive in reasonable health at lower temperatures providing accommodation is dry and frost-proof.

Description:
Size: 10 cm (4 in)
COCK:
Beak: silver. Body: grey and white with black bands around chest and breast. Wings: dark blackish-grey flecked with white. Legs: grey.
HEN:
Almost identical, but on some birds the breast appears whiter than the cock's. If mating these birds, it is best to acquire several and let them pair themselves.

Diet: (Seedeater)
Mixed millets and small plain canary seed form the basic diet. Maw and the black niger seed are two useful small seed varieties which may also be given. Grit and cuttlefish bone must always be available.

Breeding:
The Bicheno nests in a box, in an old disused nest or in a bush. It does not use much material but lines the nest with soft materials, such as feathers and wool.

The courtship dance of the cock is rather basic and consists of hopping towards the hen, turning in 180-degree circles with each hop. Part of the courtship ritual is wiping the beak on the perch.

Four to six white eggs are laid and both parents share in the incubation, never leaving the nest unattended. The sitting bird does not vacate the nest until the relief partner has entered. The cock bird is heard to sing at this time, normally a rare occurrence except in immature cock birds. The chicks hatch in 12 days and are fed by both parents. They emerge from the nest at 19 to 25 days. Soaked and sprouted seed should be fed to breeding pairs and proprietary brand canary rearing food may be purchased and can be mixed with hard boiled egg. Chopped mealworms (two or three per bird) are a useful aid.

It is an interesting sight to see a Bicheno Finch being fed by its parent on a perch. The chick raises one wing as if protecting its brothers and sisters alongside it from the parent bird. Young chicks are grey on upperparts and white below. There is no transverse band. The young birds may safely be left with their tolerant parents while a second brood is reared. They often help in the feeding of the new chicks. Young birds commence their moult at seven weeks of age and usually complete this by 16 weeks of age.

Bichenos like to roost in boxes all year round so these should be available. It is advisable in this case to segregate the sexes outside the breeding season. Plastic split rings may be used to identify the pairs for future reference.

This friendly and lively bird often forms close friendships with others and this may account for the fact that it has often hybridised with other kinds of finch.

BLACK-CHINNED YUHINA ◆
Yuhina nigrimentum
Origin: Himalayas

This is a lively, inquisitive bird that is very entertaining when it raises its small crest. It lives contentedly with sugarbirds and tanagers.

Description:
Size: 10 cm (4 in)
COCK:
Body: dark olive brown. Chest: grey-white. Stomach: buff. Crest and chin: black. Beak: brown and orange. Legs: brown.

Black-Chinned Yuhinas

HEN:
Identical so cannot be sexed by appearance. Observe behaviour to identify the cock bird. The cock is very aggressive in defence of his territory and often puts to flight birds twice his size.

Diet: (Softbill)
Fruit, including pears, grapes and sweet oranges, forms the basis of the diet. It also enjoys sponge cake soaked in a honey and water mixture and small berries. Small live insects and fine grade insectile mixture should be provided.

The Yuhina needs careful acclimatisation. It should be housed in a planted garden aviary or conservatory and needs a dry, frost-proof shelter in damp and cold weather. It can withstand fairly low temperatures, but does not tolerate damp.

Breeding:
Yuhina pairs are not keen on breeding unless housed on their own. They build nests in shrubs or climbing plants, using fine grasses and roots.

Few eggs are laid, three being the maximum. Incubation takes around 16 days. Plenty of small live insects must be provided for rearing, including fruit flies, if available, aphids, blackfly and houseflies. Mealworms and maggots are too tough skinned for this bird, but may be eaten if finely chopped.

BLACK-CRESTED BULBUL ◆
Pycnonotus melanicterus
Origin: India and Sri Lanka

The Black-Crested Bulbul is very hardy and easy to manage. A single bird can be kept in a mixed aviary with birds of

A Black-Crested Bulbul

similar size and temperament. This lively bulbul becomes very tame.

Description:
Size: 20 cm (8 in)
COCK:
Head, crest and throat: black. Breast and upper parts: olive green, fading to dull yellowish-olive on belly and around the vent. Rather striking yellow eye. Beak and legs: black.
HEN:
As cock.

Diet: (Softbill)
Proprietary brand insectile mix and fruit including apples, oranges and particularly pears and chopped grapes. It loves

berries and should have a daily allowance of livefood. Six mealworms per bird can be given each day. The insectile mix should be coarse grained rather than fine.

Breeding:
It is necessary to segregate a pair in a flight on their own. It builds a rather messy cup-shaped nest in bushy vegetation, but has been known to utilise boxes or baskets in captivity. A thickly planted area must be provided or it does not attempt to build a nest.

Two to three eggs are laid and both cock and hen share in the building of the nest and in the incubation of the eggs and rearing the young. Incubation normally lasts about 14 to 16 days and the chicks mature quickly when hatched and are ready to leave the nest after two weeks.

Successful rearing of chicks depends on the provision of plenty of livefood, mealworms, maggots, woodlice, small smooth-backed caterpillars, grasshoppers and small locusts.

Two broods per season are normal. The chicks should be removed from the parents as soon as they are able to feed themselves, or they may be attacked.

BLUE-CAPPED TANAGER ◆
Thraupis cyanocephala
Origin: North western areas of South America

Following proper acclimatisation, this colourful bird will live healthily in outdoor accommodation, becoming very hardy.

If a frost-proof shelter is provided, the Blue-Capped Tanager may winter outside or may be locked away at night depending on the weather.

A Blue-Capped Tanager

Most tanagers become quite tame with their owners and take mealworms from the hand. They are very fond of bathing and a small pool affords endless pleasure and cleans the plumage of food and droppings.

Description:
Size: 20 cm (7½ in)
COCK:
Head: cobalt-blue. Back, wings and tail: black. Underparts: dark blue. Shoulders: golden-green. Forehead and eyes: black. Rump: yellow. Beak: black. Legs: dark horn.

HEN:
Alike. Behaviour gives the best indication of sex.

Diet: (Softbill)
Soft fruits, apples, grapes, oranges, pears and bananas form a large part of the basic diet. Fine grade insectile mix should be sprinkled on the fruit. Sponge cake soaked in nectar mixture is much enjoyed. Mealworms, well-cleaned maggots, smooth, green caterpillars, grasshoppers and spiders are ideal livefood.

Breeding:
If breeding, remove this bird to a secluded, well planted aviary of its own. Wicker nest baskets should be hung in bushes in which a pair builds its open cup-shaped nest from dry grasses and roots. Two eggs form the normal clutch and the incubation period lasts 14 days. Only the hen sits on the eggs. Cock and hen both feed the chicks until they fledge between three and four weeks of age.

The parents must be provided with plenty of insects, smooth caterpillars, spiders, flies and locusts. Soft fruit, sponge cake soaked in honey mixture, finely chopped figs and dates, raisins, currants and sultanas are enjoyed. Crumbled rusks may also be mixed with fruit. Grated carrot and soaked stale bread and milk may be given. Grit, ground egg shells and some greenfood should also be fed.

As soon as the young are able to feed themselves, they should be separated from their parents before any further breeding takes place, or they may be attacked. Cock birds assume full colour at about one year of age.

(Emerald-Spotted Tanager, see page 78.)

BOURKE'S PARRAKEET □
Neophema bourkii
Origin: Central Australia

This attractive parakeet is one of the few parrotlike birds that may be safely kept in a mixed collection with small seedeaters or softbills. Its colouring is attractive despite its subdued tones. It breeds quite happily in a mixed aviary, and does not display any aggression. It does not require a large aviary, is hardy and can winter outside without heat if provided with a dry, frost-proof shelter.

Description:
Size: 23 cm (9 in)
COCK:
Beak: black. Upperparts: greyish-brown. Forehead: pale blue. Breast and underside: pinkish-brown. Wings and tail: tinged with violet blue. Legs: greyish-brown.
HEN:
Very similar, but there is little or no blue on the forehead.

Diet: (Seedeater)
Plain canary seed, mixed millets, hulled oats and groats, a small amount of sunflower seed and occasional hemp form the basic diet. Spray millet and seeding grasses are both relished and greenfood, such as dandelion and chickweed, should be offered. Grit and cuttlefish bone must always be available.

Breeding:
This species makes use of boxes or hollow logs. Three to six eggs are laid and incubation lasts about 18 days. Wood shavings or turf should be placed in the base of the nest box or log. The young are

A Bourke's Parrakeet cock

fed on the normal seed diet, but seeding grasses are eagerly taken. Plenty of greenfood should be available.

(Plum-Headed Parrakeet, see page 113. Red-Rumped Parrakeet, see page 121.)

BUDGERIGAR □ ◄
Melopsittacus undulatus
Origin: Australia

The budgerigar is one of the oldest established popular pet birds. It is very easy to manage, eager to breed, good natured and companionable. It is particularly well liked by children. It may be kept in an outdoor flight all year round, providing there is adequate shelter from cold winds.

Description:
Size: 20 cm (8 in)

COCK:
There are many different coloured budgerigars, including blue, lilac, yellow, white and variegated. The original colour of this bird is green. All colours bear a mask with black throat spots. The cock has a blue cere.

HEN:
May be distinguished by the brown cere. There is a set standard of deportment, body size and shape for those being exhibited.

Diet: (Seedeater)
Standard budgerigar mix forms the basic diet and may be purchased very easily. Millet sprays and greenfood are enjoyed. When preparing birds for breeding, add cod liver oil to seed to help prevent egg binding. Grit and cuttlefish bone must always be available.

Right: *a pair of Budgerigars*

Breeding:
When breeding it is a good idea to keep only one or two colours of budgerigar to avoid indiscriminate pairing. While peaceful with other birds, they are intolerant with others of their own kind, particularly if insufficient nest sites are available. Never keep an extra cock bird in the quarters, though an extra hen is not a problem, for she becomes a second wife. Once breeding commences, do not add further birds to the aviary or they may be attacked.

A budgerigar should not be allowed to breed before it is eight months of age, and then no more than three broods per year should be permitted.

Nest boxes should be hung in the shelter and flight, but must be protected from heavy rain. This bird tends to sit in the opening to the nest box thus preventing air from reaching its young, so make ventilation holes in the box.

During the breeding season, a pair should be given mixed millets, canary seed, sunflower seed, sweetcorn (maize), chickweed and lettuce. Willow and apple twigs are enjoyed.

More eggs are usually laid in the second clutch than in the first. The maximum number of eggs in a clutch is eight. Incubation takes about 18 days, and the cock bird feeds his hen on the nest. The young fledge after about a month and sometimes new eggs are found amongst fledglings about to leave the nest.

CALIFORNIA QUAIL　　□ ◀
Lophortyx californicus
Origin: California, U.S.A.

A very hardy and easily managed ground bird, which adds interest to the aviary at ground level and lives happily with such types as cockatiels and budgerigars or weavers, whydahs and Java Sparrows. The California Quail can be aggressive, so no more than one pair should be kept in an aviary. It must not be kept with smaller birds.

Description:
Size: 25 cm (10 in)
COCK:
Head: black and white patterned. Breast: grey. Underparts: buff with black pattern. Crest: black, angled forward. Beak: black. Legs: black.
HEN:
Lacks black and white pattern on head and has a shorter crest of brown feathers. Body as cock.

Diet: (Seedeater)
Mixed millets, crushed maize and oats, a little insectile mix, mealworms and ants' eggs form the basic diet. Other available insects should be fed and a little soaked bread is also enjoyed. Thick vegetation in the aviary encourages this bird to eat insects.

Plenty of ground cover and a dry shelter are necessary for this species. This bird is very susceptible to damp and should be enclosed in very wet weather. It likes to perch high off the ground on occasion and suitable branches should be provided in a quiet spot. California Quail, in common with other quail species, may take fright easily, particularly at night. Roosting spots should be screened with thick bushes or conifers to prevent sudden alarms.

Breeding:
In order to nest, California Quail need clumps of heather or low growing shrubs

A California Quail

and long grass. A hen is capable of laying up to 20 eggs, which she incubates alone. This hen does not always incubate her eggs properly and sometimes it may be necessary to use a domestic Bantam hen as a foster mother.

A good rearing mixture for chicks is hard boiled egg mixed with crumbled rusks. Minced raw meat, chopped green-food, ants' eggs and a variety of insects should be provided. Breadcrumbs may be added to minced meat and placed in a separate dish. Sand, grit and cuttlefish bone should be available at all times.

California Quail chicks grow rapidly and are independent in a few weeks. They may be left with their parents until the cocks attain the adult plumage of patterned colouring, when they should be removed as the cock bird may then show aggression to the other males.

(Chinese Painted Quail, see page 71.)

CANARY ■ ◇
Serinus canaria
Origin: Canary Islands

This popular song bird can be obtained in a great variety of forms and colours. The wild canary was a green colour. One of the most popular varieties is known as the Border Fancy. This is described here.

Description:

Size: 14 cm (5½ in)

COCK:

Available in a wide range of colours including yellow (buff), white, green, cinnamon. Beak: small and conical. Eyes: bold and dark. Chest: well rounded, tapering towards underparts. The stance of a good show specimen should give an angle of 60 degrees when perching. It should appear alert and lively.

HEN:

Similar, but she is usually lighter or duller in colour. The most reliable indication as to sex is the song of the cock bird. The hen merely chirps.

A Border Fancy Canary

Diet: (Seedeater)

Proprietary brand canary mixture contains a blended mix of all the necessary seeds. Some groats and niger seed may be added in cold weather. Greenfood should be supplied on a regular basis. Grit and cuttlefish bone must always be available.

Breeding:

It is most important to make sure that cock and hen are *both* in breeding condition. If either partner is not ready, any attempt at mating will prove unsuccessful.

Canary nest pans, easily purchased from pet stores, should be provided.

These are lined with felt nest liners or other soft material. Canaries also nest in square wooden nest boxes fitted with perforated zinc bases which allow plenty of cool air to circulate.

Four to five eggs are laid on consecutive days. The eggs should be removed one by one and stored, marked in number order, in a felt-lined box. Artificial eggs, purchased from pet stores, must be placed under the hen until the evening of the fourth day, when they should be removed and the real eggs replaced so she may start incubation. The incubation period is 13 to 14 days.

If the hen is reluctant to bathe, eggs should be moistened with warm water while she is off the nest feeding. Proprietary brand canary rearing food is available from pet stores and wholemeal bread and milk may be offered. Chickweed is eagerly consumed by breeding birds.

Canary chicks grow very quickly so the rearing food must be regularly increased in quantity. Within 16 to 20 days, chicks are ready to leave the nest. They are dependent on their parents for food for a further ten days. By the time the brood is fully independent, the hen is usually ready to lay again.

Canaries are often cross-bred with certain British finches to produce attractive hybrids known as 'mules'.

CEDAR WAXWING
Bombycilla cedrorum
Origin: North America

This is an easy-to-manage softbill, although watch out for a tendency to gain weight. It needs a large aviary and a carefully regulated diet. The smooth, silky plumage of the Cedar Waxwing is one of its most notable features. It is placid in nature and thrives well in groups. Several pairs may be kept together and with other species of similar size. If tame and steady, this bird makes an excellent exhibition species.

Description:
Size: 15 cm (6 in)
COCK:
Head: pink-olive merging into grey-brown. Back and upper breast as head. Rump: grey. Tail: grey and edged with yellow. Eye stripe: wide black band. White streaks under eye. Wings: black with bright red flashes. Crest: pink-olive. Beak: black. Legs: black.
HEN:
Alike, so it cannot be sexed by appearance. Observe behaviour to identify a cock bird.

Diet: (Softbill)
Coarse grade insectile mix, soaked currants and sultanas, raisins and apples should be provided. It also enjoys berries.

Encourage exercise by siting food and drinking vessels some distance away from favourite perching spots.

Breeding:
It is considered quite difficult to breed these birds, so try to keep several pairs. The aviary needs to be well planted: bushy conifers with high-mounted, cup-shaped wicker baskets and open-topped nest boxes set in the thickest foliage, encourage nesting.

Successful hatching of chicks requires hard work by the owner, as the parents must have a plentiful supply of insects including gnats, flies and mosquitoes. Outside the breeding season, the Cedar Waxwing shows less interest in livefood.

CHESTNUT-BREASTED FINCH ○ ■

Lonchura castaneothorax
Origin: Australia

This Australian finch is beautifully marked and its plumage is glossy and smooth. It is easy to keep and quite hardy. This species does well in a medium sized aviary and mixes amicably with other seedeaters of similar size.

Description:
Size: 10 to 13 cm (4 to 5 in)

COCK:
Head: black. Chest: chestnut with a black band above stomach. Stomach: creamy-beige. Shoulders, wings and tail: dark chestnut. Legs: grey. Beak: blue-grey. Eyes: black.

HEN:
Identical, but the cock sings and the hen does not.

Diet: (Seedeater)
Plain canary seed, mixed millets, green-food and a little livefood form the basic diet. Grit and cuttlefish bone must always be available. This species can be lethargic

A group of Cedar Waxwings

A Chestnut-Breasted Finch

and has a tendency to put on weight, so do not overfeed.

Breeding:
This species makes a very attentive parent, but should not be allowed to breed at a very early age. Chestnut-Breasted cock birds also show a preference for Bengalese hens if housed with this species, so do not mix them if you wish to avoid cross-breeding. Nest boxes should be placed in the aviary and try to provide some grass clippings, so that the pair may fill their chosen site. The nest is filled to

overflowing and the eggs laid precariously on top.

Five or six large white eggs form the normal clutch. After three or four eggs are laid, both parents share incubation which takes 13 days.

Provide hard-boiled egg, insectile mix and soaked and sprouted seed for the parents to rear their brood. The young chicks become rather nervous as they grow and great care should be taken when they are about 18 to 22 days old, as they sometimes leave the nest too early if alarmed, which may prove fatal.

The Chestnut-Breasted Finch does not roost in nest boxes, so ensure that they are in the shelter by nightfall in colder weather. This species has a tendency to overgrown claws, so try to clip them at least three or four times a year.

CHINESE PAINTED QUAIL ●○■
Excalfactoria chinensis   *(in colour*
Origin: Southern Asia   *page 27)*

This is a beautiful miniature quail which prospers well in a mixed aviary in company with other small birds. It performs a useful service by eating waste seed from the ground. Only one pair of Chinese Painted Quail should be kept per aviary, as they are intolerant of their own kind and fighting may occur.

Description:
Size: 13 cm (5 in)
COCK:
Head: mottled with a black and white pattern. Body: brown mottled with black and beige. Breast: blue-grey. Beak: black. Legs: yellow.
HEN:
Body: dull brown, mottled with black.

Breast: pale brown. Lacks patterned head of the cock.

Diet: (Seedeater)

Mixed millets and plain canary seed form the basic diet. Maw seed is also enjoyed. Greenfood should be given and some livefood, preferably small insects. The Chinese Painted Quail forages actively in the aviary for insects. An area of thick grass should be provided; this will give the bird a supply of insects and also a source of cover.

During cold weather this species should be placed in an indoor enclosure, but does not require heat.

Breeding:

A shallow hollow in the ground, concealed in thick vegetation, forms the nest site. Moss and leaves and blades of grass are placed in the depression to line the nest. Take care not to trample on the nest when entering the aviary.

The hen lays between six and eight eggs and incubates them alone, while the cock guards the nest against any interference, ferociously if needs be. The incubation period is 16 days. Upon hatching the chicks are immediately able to run about. At this age they can slip through even very small mesh. Place a board about 10 cm (4 in) around the bottom sides of their aviary to prevent this.

The chicks eat ants' eggs, finely chopped mealworms and lettuce. Insectile mix should be provided and sometimes a little raw minced meat. Chopped hard-boiled egg is also useful, but remains must be cleared away before they spoil. The young also need plenty of ground egg shell, lime and grit.

The cock may not adapt well to fatherhood and may worry the hen while she is sitting on the eggs, or peck at the young chicks when they first appear. This sometimes happens with the first brood and can be attributed to inexperience. Should this happen, it is wise to remove the cock from the aviary. At four weeks the chicks are independent and should be taken away and the cock returned. The pair nest again for a second round. Pairs do not always rear well in their first season.

No more than three broods of chicks per year should be allowed. Segregate the cock if he attempts persistent breeding.

(California Quail, see page 66.)

COCKATIEL

Nymphicus hollandicus
Origin: Australia

(in colour page 90)

The Cockatiel is easy to house, feed and breed. It is also a very gentle bird and may be kept with other compatible species including small finches. When breeding, however, it should have its own accommodation, preferably with a large wooden nest box hung in a quiet corner of the flight. The Cockatiel needs a long flight since it is a strong flyer and needs ample space to exercise its wings.

Description:

Size: 33 cm (13 in)
COCK:
Several different colour forms exist, including a Lutino variety.
Upperparts: dark grey. Under surfaces: light grey and yellowish bluff. Front of head and crest, cheeks and throat: bright yellow. Ear coverts: orange. A striking white band runs down the centre of the wings. Beak and legs: dark grey.

HEN:
Similar, but underside of tail is barred with yellow and grey. The yellow on the face is duller than on the cock.

Diet: (Seedeater)
Plain canary seed, mixed millets and a little sunflower and hemp seed form the basic diet. Fresh greenfood and fruit such as apple and pear, should be provided. Plentiful supplies of grit and cuttlefish bone are essential.

Breeding:
The Cockatiel is a prolific breeder and goes to nest three times in a season. Six or more eggs may be laid in one clutch. Breeding pairs should be fed on soaked seed and bread and milk to produce top quality chicks. Both parents share in the incubation of the eggs which takes from 19 to 21 days. The young fledge between four and five weeks.

CORDON BLEU WAXBILL ●○
Uraeginthus bengalus　　*(in colour*
Origin: Central Africa　　*page 87)*

This is a popular member of the waxbill family which lives for many years in an aviary after proper acclimatisation. It is highly recommended for the novice fancier. Several pairs of these birds can be kept in a collection of waxbills. The Cordon Bleu is not aggressive, even when breeding.

Description:
Size: 10 cm (4 in)
COCK:
Body: greyish-fawn. Undersides: blue. Head: blue. Cheeks: red crescent-shaped patches. Beak: pinky-grey. Legs: biege.

HEN:
Similar, but easy to sex since she lacks the red cheek patches.

Diet: (Seedeater)
Mixed millets and plain canary seed form the basic diet. Greenfood is always welcomed and millet sprays are enjoyed. Grit and cuttlefish bone must always be given.

While this bird becomes hardy outside, it suffers from sudden changes in temperature and from damp. In winter, try to house the Cordon Bleu in an indoor flight or in a cage in a moderately warm room.

Breeding:
The cock bird displays to the hen by means of an amusing dance with a straw in his beak, and a pleasant song.

The Cordon Bleu is usually free breeding. A pair builds a nest in a bush using any material it can find. Some fanciers provide open-fronted nest boxes or globular wicker baskets.

The hen weaves an intricate nest which is lined with soft grasses and feathers, some of which she plucks from the cock's breast. The hen lays a number of eggs, normally between four and seven. Both parents take turns in sitting for the incubation period of 14 days.

Small livefood is necessary to rear the chicks successfully, including ants' eggs and mealworms. Insectile mix, seeding grasses, and egg food are welcomed. Sponge cake soaked in a honey and water mixture may be welcome.

The Cordon Bleu has been known to breed with the similar Blue-Breasted Waxbill, the St. Helena Waxbill and even with Bengalese.
(Golden-Breasted, see page 79. Orange-Cheeked, see page 104. Red-Eared, see page 120. Violet-Eared, see page 132.)

CUT-THROAT FINCH ◄

Amadina fasciata *(in colour*
Origin: Africa *page 82)*

This extremely hardy finch will live in an outside aviary for many years. It is sometimes inclined to be aggressive and should only be kept with large sized birds. It is easy to manage in all other respects and makes a good addition to a mixed collection.

Description:

Size: 13 cm (5 in)

COCK:

Body: Beige-brown dappled with dark greyish-black, looking like scales. Beak: grey. Legs: dull pink. Throat: scarlet.

HEN:

Similar, but she lacks the scarlet throat patch.

Diet: (Seedeater)

Mixed millets, plain canary seed and seeding grasses form the basic diet. Greenfood is appreciated. Grit and cuttlefish bone must always be available for this species.

This bird may be kept out of doors all year round, needing only a dry, frost-proof shelter to which it can retire in cold weather.

Breeding:

In display, the Cut-Throat cock sings a quiet little song, ruffling his throat feathers as he sings. A nest is built from grasses, roots, hairs or any available material, preferably inside a nest box. It is normally lined with feathers. The hen lays four to six eggs which both parents take turns to incubate. The young are normally hatched after 12 days' incubation. Rearing food should consist of soaked and sprouted seeds, soaked stale bread, a few mealworms and fresh ants' eggs. Nest inspection is resented while the parents are sitting.

During the breeding season it is a good idea to mix cod liver oil with the birds' seed, since this helps prevent egg binding to which Cut-Throat hens are often prone. In cold weather, the same measure may be taken to ensure health and vitality. Another aid during the breeding season is sponge cake soaked in honey and a little fine grade insectile mix.

DIAMOND DOVE ○■

Geopelia c. cuneata *(in colour*
Origin: Australia *page 82)*

The Diamond Dove is particularly suitable for keeping with seedeaters in a mixed collection. It is a useful ground bird which eats seed on the floor that might otherwise go to waste. It is one of the smallest of the dove family, but is intolerant of other doves of any type, so only one pair is recommended per aviary. This bird may also be seen perching in bushes off the ground.

Description:

Size: 18 cm (7½ in)

COCK:

Head, neck and breast: pale silver-grey. Nape and back: pale brown. Wing coverts: dark grey with a round white spot near each feathertip. Tail: central feathers dark grey with black towards the tips. Eyes: orange-yellow or red. Eye ring: bright coral red. Beak: olive brown. Legs and feet: red.

HEN:

Similar, but slightly smaller with a thinner head. During the breeding season the hen's eye ring is a paler red. At other times, the clearest indication as to sex is the cock's fascinating display with spread tail.

Diet: (Seedeater)
Mixed millets, plain canary seed and maw seed in small quantities form the basic diet. It also enjoys insectile mixture, an occasional mealworm, ants' eggs and greenfood, particularly chopped young cabbage leaves. Grit must always be available.

The Diamond Dove can be housed outside all year round, but needs a dry place to roost. As this species may take fright after dark and injure itself or others, it needs an enclosed shelter for safety.

Breeding:
The Diamond Dove prefers nest pans or shallow boxes for nesting. These are filled with twigs, coarse grass and moss. The cock displays eagerly to the hen by dancing around her, while fanning out his tail and beating his wings on the ground.

Two eggs are the normal clutch and from these a cock and hen emerge. Both parents take turns on sitting on the eggs for the 13-day incubation period. Rearing food should consist of sprouted seeds and soaked bread. Once the chicks are independent they should be removed from their parents otherwise they are chased away when a new round of eggs is laid.

Brothers and sisters may be paired together when adult. This does no harm but they should not be paired often or inbreeding may result, impairing the quality of the young.

(Laughing Dove, see page 98.)

DIAMOND SPARROW
Staganopleura guttata
Origin: Australia

The colourful Diamond Sparrow is one of the most easily bred Australian finches. A pair in a mixed collection may be well behaved towards the other inhabitants or very aggressive, for individual temperaments vary greatly in this species.

Description:
Size: 13 cm (5 in)
COCK:
Head: grey. Throat: white. Back: grey. Sides: black dotted with white spots. Black band on chest. Rump: scarlet. Belly: white. Legs: grey. Beak: red.
HEN:
Similar in appearance, but the hen has a paler red rim around the eye than the cock. The cock bird's song is a short rasping note and the hen merely chirps.

Diet: (Seedeater)
Small plain canary seed and mixed millets form the basic diet, with some greenfood. Grit and cuttlefish bone must always be available.

Since this bird spends much of its time on the ground, it should be shut inside the shelter during very heavy rain to prevent chills.

Breeding:
The display of the cock is the best indication of the bird's sex. He approaches the hen holding a long grass stalk in his beak whilst fully stretching his neck upwards, then lowers his head until his beak almost touches his chest and hops closer to the hen in an ungainly fashion. Although the hen usually looks bored with his antics,

this signifies that she has accepted him as her mate. If the hen is not interested she flies off.

Diamond Sparrows nest in half-fronted nest boxes in which they construct their own domed nest. Pairs re-arrange the nest several times until it is considered perfect. The hen often plucks white feathers from her own breast to line the nest.

Six eggs form the maximum clutch and both parents incubate the eggs. On changing over, the sitters call out to each other with a strange snore-like noise. They commence sitting as soon as the first egg is laid.

Offer as much livefood as possible during breeding, including fresh ants' eggs and boiled mealworms, finely chopped with a plentiful supply of grit.

The chicks are easily reared and leave the nest in 22 to 24 days. In the first few weeks they return to the nest to be fed and to sleep. Nest inspection is not usually resented by Diamond Sparrows. Once independent the young should be removed from their intolerant parents unless the aviary is very large. The young moult out between seven and 13 weeks of age.

Diamond Sparrows who go to nest too young should have their chicks removed for fostering by Bengalese. Do not place more than three young chicks with one pair of Bengalese, since Diamond Sparrow chicks eat particularly large quantities of food.

Diamond Sparrows have a habit of plucking each other and also sometimes their neighbours, so should be watched for this bad habit.

Once the initial difficulty of obtaining

A Diamond Sparrow

a true pair is overcome, breeding results should be good.

(Java Sparrow, see page 97. Yellow Sparrow, see page 134.)

ELEGANT GRASS PARRAKEET ☐
Neophema elegans
Origin: South and West Australia

(in colour page 83)

The Elegant Grass Parrakeet may be kept safely with other birds, except during the breeding season when it is wiser to house it alone, unless in a large aviary.

Description:
Size: 23 cm (9 in)
COCK:
Body: olive green. Forehead: bears a deep cobalt-blue band, edged with light blue. Wings: exhibit these same two shades on their edges. Throat and chest: greenish-yellow. Belly: yellow. Beak: charcoal grey. Legs: greyish-brown.
HEN:
Similar, but all the colour tones are much paler so they can be sexed easily.

Diet: (Seedeater)
Mixed millets and plain canary seed with a small amount of sunflower and hemp seed form the basic diet. Seeding grasses, regular supplies of greenfood, grit and cuttlefish bone should be provided.

This bird is easily managed and does not require a large flight unless kept with others for breeding. A sunny, warm aviary suits it well but some shade is necessary to prevent sun stroke. A dry, frostproof shelter should be provided for cold weather. It is not quite as hardy as some parrotlike species.

Breeding:

Place nest boxes and hollow logs in the accommodation. The Elegant Grass Parrakeet requires a slightly larger nest box than a budgerigar. The cock bird's courtship display is amusing to watch as he performs a head bobbing dance accompanied by a twittering song.

The hen lays four to five eggs which she incubates for 18 to 21 days. Sprouted seed should be provided for the parents to rear the brood. This is the only necessary addition to the normal seed diet. Parents even rear their young on hard seed.

Chicks are ready to leave the nest in approximately 28 to 34 days. Young Elegant Grass Parrakeets are very shy when they first leave the nest, so make sure there are plenty of bushes in the aviary to provide cover for the timid youngsters and they soon gain confidence.

(Splendid, see page 125. Turquoisine, see page 130.)

EMERALD-SPOTTED TANAGER ◆
Tangara guttata   (*in colour*
Origin: South America   *page 87)*

An attractive, small tanager of slightly more delicate constitution than some of the larger types, it requires correct feeding and a high standard of cleanliness. It is not a difficult bird to keep, but extra care and attention are important.

Description:

Size: 13 cm (5 in)
COCK:
Body: bright green. Underparts: white with dark flecks. Head: spotted with

black. Breast: green spotted with black. Beak: upper mandible, black; lower mandible, beige. Legs: grey.
HEN:
Similar, but lacks the yellow on forehead and around eyes. Sometimes a little larger than the cock. Colour of body more grey-green than the cock.

Diet: (Softbill)

Apples, pears, sweet oranges and grapes form the basic diet. Sponge caked soaked in nectar mixture is enjoyed. Fine grade insectile mix should be used to coat diced fruit. Some livefood should be given including mealworms and well cleaned maggots.

Careful acclimatisation is needed and it is necessary to house this species inside during the winter months. Alternatively, it may be kept in a heated conservatory throughout the year. It should be sprayed regularly with a mist spray to keep plumage in good condition and free from food and droppings.

Breeding:

Breeding may be difficult, so encourage a pair by housing them in a well-planted aviary with plants which are difficult to destroy, such as the tough-leaved Cheese Plant (*Monstera*). Both the cock and hen share in building the cup-shaped nest. A base may be provided in the form of canary nest pans or wicker baskets suspended from tall plants.

Two eggs are normally laid and the hen sits alone for the 14-day incubation period. The chicks are dependent on their parents for about three weeks. Try to offer plenty of livefood, such as mealworms, spiders, maggots and smooth caterpillars. Soft fruits and soaked dried fruit, such as currants, raisins, sultanas, figs and dates, are enjoyed and may be dusted with fine grade insectile mix. Fresh ants' eggs are eagerly accepted and greenfood should also be offered. The young should be separated from their parents as soon as they are seen to be feeding themselves, so that another round may be bred.

(Blue-Capped, see page 62.)

GOLDEN-BREASTED ●
WAXBILL
Estrilda subflava
Origin: West Africa

A neat and lively small waxbill, this bird can be kept with ease in a mixed collection of waxbills and small finches.

Description:
Size: 10 cm (5 in)
COCK:
Body: olive grey and dark yellow. Sides: grey with fine yellow wavy lines. Eyebrows: red stripe. Legs: cream.
HEN:
Similar, but paler underneath, slightly smaller and lacking red eyebrow stripes.

Diet: (Seedeater)
Mixed millets, plain canary seed, millet sprays and seeding grasses are enjoyed. Greenfood, a few mealworms or cleaned maggots, grit and cuttlefish bone should be provided.

Try to bring these birds indoors or provide a dry warm shelter away from any draughts in cold weather.

Breeding:
The Golden-Breasted Waxbill may be intolerant, both of its own kind and of

A Golden-Breasted Waxbill

other species, when nesting. This should not normally amount to more than chasing other birds away from the nest site. It does not interfere with other birds that are nesting.

The cock's mating song, a rather monotonous chirping, can be heard from early in the morning until dusk. He performs a dainty courtship dance.

Globular wicker nest baskets and open-fronted nest boxes may be provided. A pair may also build their own nest using various materials, including hair, wool teasings and feathers. Plenty of plant cover is needed to encourage these birds to breed.

Three to five white eggs are laid which, if fertile, should hatch in 11 to 12 days. The hen may tend to lay eggs all year

A Golden-Fronted Fruitsucker

round but often the eggs prove to be infertile. Both parents share in the incubation.

Breeding birds should be fed plenty of small livefood, sprouted seeds, mashed hard-boiled egg yolk, fresh ants' eggs and fine grade insectile mix.

The young fledge with yellowish-grey body colour, yellowish-red tail feathers and black beaks.

(Cordon Bleu, see page 73. Orange-Cheeked, see page 104. Red-Eared, see page 120. Violet-Eared, see page 132.)

GOLDEN-FRONTED △
FRUITSUCKER
Chloropsis aurifrons
Origin: Himalayas and Burma

One of the most colourful softbills available, this supremely graceful bird also has a delightful, melodious song. It soon becomes tame and eagerly takes a daily mealworm from the hand. It makes an excellent show bird and is often a very clever mimic of other birds. It is best kept with birds of similar size in a well-sized, planted aviary.

Description:
Size: 20 cm (8 in)
COCK:
Body: bright green, shoulder patch of turquoise-blue. Head: gold on crown. Side of head and neck: black. Cheeks sport a blue band. Underside: light green. Tail: green and navy blue. Beak: black. Legs: dark green.
HEN:
Similar, but slightly duller colours.

Diet: (Softbill)
Most fruits, including pear, orange, banana and grapes, form the basic diet.

Try scooping out an orange and refilling the centre with coarse grade insectile mix and orange pieces, and watch this bird delight in dipping into it. It loves to suck the juice from a halved orange. Raisins, chopped dates, currants and sultanas are all eagerly taken. Mealworms and well-cleaned maggots are among the most suitable livefood for this species and other insects should be provided as available. Egg yolk and minced meat are very suitable additions to the diet. Food should be placed on a pedestal high off the ground to keep it clean as this bird often treads around in dishes. The Golden-Fronted Fruitsucker often carries a morsel of food to a favourite perching spot and daintily consumes it.

This bird is aggressive with its own kind so only a sole bird or a known true pair should be kept. It does not cause problems when housed with other species.

Breeding:
A pair will go to nest more readily if housed alone. When nesting, pairs build cup-shaped nests high up in trees or shrubs as they need great privacy. Few eggs are laid, probably two at a maximum. Breeding birds should be fed plenty of soft fruits, insects and sponge cake soaked in honey and water.

This species loves to bathe and should, if possible, have a small pool or bird bath. It enjoys flicking raindrops from wet foliage on to its plumage.

All types of fruitsucker should be carefully acclimatised. Although it becomes quite hardy in time, it is advisable to house the Golden-Fronted Fruitsucker in a conservatory in winter, as it cannot tolerate frost.

GOLDFINCH ■ ◇
Carduelis carduelis (in colour
Origin: UK/Europe page 91)

The Goldfinch has been kept and bred by numerous fanciers in Great Britain for centuries. It is noted for its soft, sweet song and is always tame and friendly. It thrives well when housed with canaries in a mixed collection.

Description:
Size: 13 cm (5 in)
COCK:
Eyes: light brown. Beak: light cream, blackish on tip. Mask: red edged with white, the red often fades in aviary specimens. Crown, side of neck and wings: black. Wings also show bands of yellow and white spots at tips of flights. Back: brown. Upper tail coverts: buff. Underparts: white, tinged with brown. Tail: black with white edges. Feet and legs: light brown.
HEN:
Very similar, but the mask is slightly smaller and a duller red. Sometimes a little difficult to sex by appearance.

Diet: (Seedeater)
Niger is the most favoured seed. Canary mixture, oats, groats and some hulled sunflower seed should also be given. It also enjoys hemp, but sunflower seed is a ready substitute in countries where hemp is illegal. Greenfood is enjoyed and thistles are relished by this species. Grit and cuttlefish bone must always be provided.

Breeding:
This species is usually rather keen to breed. Pairs make neat, compact, small nests with dried grasses, hair, wool and

Above: *a pair of Cut-Throat Finches*
Right: *a Diamond Dove cock*
Far right: *an Elegant Grass Parrakeet*

feathers. Four to six eggs are laid and the incubation period is 13 days. The hen sits alone but parents share in feeding the young. Two nests per year can be expected from pairs.

Cock Goldfinches also mate readily with other British finches and canaries producing attractive hybrids and colourful mules.

GOULDIAN FINCH ○■
Chloebia gouldiae, sometimes known as
Poephila gouldiae   (*in colour*
Origin: Northern Australia   *page 95*)

A particularly colourful, beautiful species of finch which exhibits well and is peaceful with other species. It can be housed outdoors during the summer months, but is best housed indoors unless kept in a warm climate. A mean temperature of 15°C (60°F) should be maintained for best results. Although it can be acclimatised to live without heat, it must always be protected from draughts. It is often lethargic so should be encouraged to take exercise by placing perches some distance apart.

Description:
Size: 13 cm (5 in)
Three colour forms exist: the Red-Headed Gouldian, Black-Headed Gouldian and Yellow-Headed Gouldian. There is also a White-Breasted mutation. Basic colours of the description are the same, as only the head colour differs.
Example: Red-Headed Gouldian.
COCK:
Lower neck, mantle and wings: green. Chest: bright purple. Lower breast and stomach: saffron-yellow. Back of head and rump: lilac. Face and head: red

bordered with black. Beak: cream. Legs: flesh colour.
HEN:
Similar, but her chest is pale mauve. Other colours are slightly duller. Adult birds are easy to sex. Since Gouldians are reputed to be difficult to keep alive, only fully moulted out, adult specimens should be purchased for breeding purposes.

Diet: (Seedeater)
Best quality mixed millets and small plain canary seed form the basic diet. Proprietary brand foreign finch mix may be purchased for this bird. Greenfood is desirable, but is not always taken, and grit and flaked cuttlefish bone are essential. Granulated charcoal should also be provided, as it is enjoyed by this species. Many fanciers prefer to feed soaked or sprouted seed both during and outside the breeding season. The Gouldian Finch should always be given cold, boiled tap water to drink.

Breeding:
The courtship dance of the Gouldian Finch is interesting to watch: he jumps up and down on the perch trilling to his hen, who, if agreeable, quivers her tail in response.

Open-fronted nest boxes with light entrances, or globular wicker baskets, are accepted as nest sites. Some pairs make fine nests from long grasses inside the box while others carry very little nesting material inside.

Six eggs are normally laid and both parents take turns in the incubation after the third egg is laid. The young hatch in 16 days. The chicks have luminous mouth spots to aid their parents in feeding inside the dark of the nest. The hen sits in the nest with the chicks while the cock guards the entrance.

Parents rear their chicks with the aid of brown bread soaked in milk and/or soaked and sprouted seed.

Young Gouldians are coloured grey at first and do not attain full mature colour until almost a year of age. The juvenile moult is particularly difficult for this species. They should not be fed entirely on hard seed until they have gone through this moult.

The Gouldian should not be bred until fully adult (usually one year). Hens assume a black cast on the tip of the beak when ready for breeding. Pair bonding is very strong in this species. Separate pairs after breeding each year to give them a rest, but make sure the bird is reunited with the correct partner.

Sometimes this species is afflicted with a condition known as 'twirling', which only seems to occur in Gouldians. The bird swings its head and neck around in a circular fashion. This can lead to premature death. Never use such a bird for breeding. The cause is not certain but may be attributed to in-breeding.

GREEN CARDINAL ◀ ◇
Gubernatrix cristata
Origin: Brazil and Argentina

A single bird can be kept quite safely in a mixed collection. However, pairs need to be watched to make sure there is no fighting. Although less colourful than the Red-Crested and Pope Cardinal, the Green Cardinal is often more eager to breed.

Description:
Size: 20 cm (8 in)

A Green Cardinal

Left: *an Emerald-Spotted Tanager*
Far left: *a Green Singing Finch*
Below: *a pair of Cordon Bleus*

COCK:
Body: olive green with black markings. Cheeks and throat: yellow. Crest and throat patch: black. Stomach: greenish-yellow. Beak: grey. Legs: dark grey.
HEN:
Body: grey-green and greyish-white. The cock and hen of this species are quite dissimilar and may be sexed fairly easily.

Diet: (Seedeater)
Plain canary seed, mixed millets, sunflower seed and hemp form the basic diet. Some livefood, fruit tree twigs, grit and cuttlefish bone should be provided for this species.

This hardy species can tolerate low temperatures, but not damp conditions. It is easy to keep in a medium sized aviary with a dry, damp-proof shelter for cold weather.

Breeding:
Pairs construct a nest in a fairly dense bush or shrub. An open-fronted nest box, a basket or a cup-shaped receptacle should be provided to encourage breeding. Plenty of livefood should be given including small, smooth caterpillars, woodlice, spiders, fresh ants' eggs, wasp grubs and a few mealworms and maggots.

Three to four eggs form a normal clutch although as many as six are sometimes laid. Chicks fledge after four weeks and are normally independent in a further two weeks. Sprouted seeds and seeding grass heads should be fed to the chicks. Remove the young from their parents as soon as they are seen to be eating well on their own.

(Pope Cardinal, see page 113. Red-Crested Cardinal, see page 119.)

GREEN SINGING FINCH ●○■
Serinus mozambicus   (in colour
Origin: Africa   page 86)

This finch is a superb and popular, easy-to-manage song bird which is a distant relative of the canary. It is hardy and lives for a very long time, maybe attaining as much as 20 years of age.

Description:
Size: 10 to 13 cm (4 to 5 in)
COCK:
Head: grey. Neck and back: grey-green. Chin, throat and belly: yellow. Eyebrows: bright yellow with yellow patches on sides of chin. Wings and tail: black. There is a yellow edge to some of the wing feathers. Eyes: encircled with black stripe. Beak and legs: cream-grey.
HEN:
Similar, but easy to distinguish since she also sports a collar of black spots.

Diet: (Seedeater)
Plain canary seed and yellow millet form the staple diet. Spray millet is also much appreciated. Greenfood should be provided regularly and an occasional apple is enjoyed. Grit and cuttlefish bone must always be available.

This finch may be kept outside all year round but should have a dry, frost-proof shelter in which to roost.

This species does not require a large aviary since it is rarely seen to fly a great deal. If several pairs are kept, they usually all roost together at night on one single perch high in the shelter.

Breeding:
Nests are built in shrubs or trees or an open-fronted nest box. The hen is re-

sponsible for constructing the nest and incubating the eggs. The incubation period is 13 days. While the hen is nest building and sitting, the cock perches nearby, singing frequently. During the incubation period, he sits close by the nest like a sentry on duty.

Breeding birds should be fed plenty of sprouted seed, grass seed and greenfood. They also benefit from finely chopped mealworms, egg and ants' eggs.

The younger are independent 21 days after leaving the best. The cock feeds the young for several weeks afterwards, but they should be removed from their parents before further breeding takes place.

As well as breeding with its own kind, a cock may be mated with a small canary hen to produce an attractive mule.

Cock and hen Green Singing Finches show little interest in remaining together after the breeding season is over. The cock bird can be aggressive with its companions when breeding, but at other times is tolerant and peaceful, although there may be an occasional squabble with its mate out of the breeding season.

Occasionally this species may be found to be suffering from sore eyes caused by wiping its face on a dirty perch. It appears short-sighted and may frequently have difficulty in finding the feed dish. Regular cleaning of perches prevents this problem.

GREEN TWINSPOT ● ○ ■
Mandingoa nitidula
Origin: East Africa

This is not an easy bird to establish and its management is difficult for the inexperienced fancier. It is a rather delicate species, which always needs more care than

A Green Twinspot

Left: *a Yellow-backed Whydah*
Below left: *an Andaman Mynah*
Below right: *a Lutino Cockatiel*
Right: *a Goldfinch*

most other types of seedeater. It is, however, a striking, attractive bird, which agrees well with most types of small waxbill, though breeding results are better if a pair is housed alone.

Description:
Size: 10 cm (4 in)
COCK:
Body: olive green. Breast and stomach: black with white spots. Facial mask: orange-red. Beak: black. Legs: cream.
HEN:
Similar, but its facial mask is golden beige.

Diet: (Seedeater)
Mixed millets form the staple diet. Millet sprays are enjoyed and livefood is also necessary. Mealworms and maggots may be fed, if available, and spiders and small smooth caterpillars are very popular with this species. Grit and cuttlefish bone must always be available.

Breeding:
The cock performs his courtship display on the ground, dancing round the hen with a feather in his beak. The hen responds by wagging her tail sideways.

A pair should be provided with globular, wicker baskets hung in a well planted aviary. During the breeding season this bird must have livefood and only rears young if plenty of insects are provided. The aviary should be well protected from inclement weather at all times.

An average clutch of eggs numbers three. The incubation period is 13 days and both parents take turns in sitting. Egg rearing food, soaked seed and soaked bread are useful for helping to feed the young. They fledge in three weeks.

(Peter's Twinspot, see page 108.)

INDIAN BLUE ROLLER
Coracias benghalensis
Origin: Asia

This medium sized softbill may be kept in harmony in a large aviary with other species, particularly jays, and several members of its own kind, providing that all rollers in a collection are introduced to their accommodation together. This bird is not aggressive with smaller species, despite its heavy build. However, it does sometimes emit rather harsh grating sounds which may not endear one to the neighbours! Fortunately, it usually only makes a noise at the beginning of the breeding season.

Description:
Size: 46 cm (13 in)
COCK:
Body: Greyish-blue and lilac. Head: turquoise-grey. Wings: turquoise and royal blue. Chest and cheeks: lavender. Throat: buff. Underparts: lavender fading to pale brown. The head appears very large.
HEN
Very similar so cannot be sexed by appearance. Observe behaviour to distinguish between sexes.

Diet: (Softbill)
Course grade insectile mix, minced meat and mealworms form the basic diet. Locusts and crickets are relished. As much insect food as possible must be provided.

The name 'roller' comes from the bird's habit of flying up high and swooping downwards with fast beating wings in a rolling type motion. This is normally observed only at the start of the breeding

An Indian Blue Roller

season. At other times this species appears quite lethargic, although this is deceptive since it can spot an insect and catch it with great speed. This bird particularly enjoys basking in sunshine on a high thin branch.

Breeding:

Few breeding results have been recorded in captivity, as it is often difficult to obtain a true pair. Try to purchase several birds as they may then form a pair themselves.

Nesting takes place high up in trees so it is difficult to provide the correct conditions in an aviary. Plenty of cover is required in order to make the birds feel secure.

INDIAN ZOSTEROPS ●◆
Zosterops palpebrosa   *(in colour*
Origin: India   *page 19)*

This warbler-like bird readily becomes tame and is a good exhibition species.

Description:
Size: 10 cm (4 in)
COCK
Body: green. Breast: grey-white. Belly: grey-white. Chin: yellow. Throat: yellow. Eye ring: white feathers. Beak: black. Legs: grey.
HEN:
Similar, but these birds may be sexed by the attractive song of the cock bird.

Left: *an African Silverbill*
Right: *a Black-Headed Gouldian Finch cock with a Red-Headed hen*
Below: *a Laughing Dove*

Diet: (Softbill)

The basic diet consists of fruit, especially pears, oranges and grapes, fine grade insectile mix and sponge cake soaked in a honey and water mixture. Small livefood is necessary, including mealworms, cleaned maggots, spiders and flies. This bird also enjoys crumbled rusks with grated carrot and finely chopped dates. Nectar should be available in drinkers at all times.

The delicate appearance of this bird is deceptive since it is surprisingly hardy and, once acclimatised, can winter successfully outside if there is access to a frost-proof shelter.

Breeding:

If conditions are right, Indian Zosterops make good parents. Since these birds are difficult to sex, try to keep several in the aviary and a pair should become evident.

Breeding may be encouraged with an artificial nest, placed in a nest box. This may be added to by the pair. Sometimes, they construct a nest using grasses, roots and wool. Three to four pale turquoise, narrow eggs are laid. There are no flecks on the shells.

Plenty of live insects are needed to rear a nest of chicks, including greenfly, blackfly and spiders. Nests are usually located high up in the aviary.

JAPANESE HAWFINCH
Eophona personata
Origin: Japan

A seedeater with fairly simple requirements, this hardy species soon makes itself at home in a well-planted aviary, although it may at first be shy. It enjoys roosting in trees of the evergreen variety.

Despite the heavy beak, typical of the hawfinch family, it is peaceful and non-aggressive, but should be housed with birds of similar size, not smaller.

Its attractive, glossy plumage makes it a very handsome specimen and its immaculate appearance is maintained throughout the year, even when moulting. It is an excellent bird for exhibition.

Description:

Size: 20 cm (8 in)

COCK

Head and throat: black. Neck: blue-grey. Belly: reddish-brown. Rump: white. Wings: black, barred with white. Tail: black. Beak: yellow with lilac patch at base. The tip of the beak is black. Legs: pink.

HEN:

Paler in colour. Head and throat: grey. Beak: yellow.

Diet: (Seedeater)

Plain canary seed, sunflower seed, a little hemp seed and some buckwheat form the basic diet. Regular supplies of greenfood and some livefood are much appreciated. Grit and cuttlefish bone must alwyas be available.

Breeding:

A pair of these birds may be encouraged to begin nesting in a wicker nest basket. The basket should be tied securely in a position with plenty of cover. Sometimes a pair builds a nest. A maximum of four eggs form the normal clutch and the hen sits alone for the 14-day incubation period. At this time, the pair should be supplied with plenty of livefood, such as maggots, mealworms and small smooth caterpillars. Canary rearing food and extra greenfood are very beneficial.

A Japanese Hawfinch

JAVA SPARROW ◄ ◇
Padda oryzivora
Origin: Indonesia

This hardy species may live for many years with the minimum of care and attention. Once acclimatised, the Java Sparrow can be kept in an outside aviary all year round.

The smooth shiny plumage of the Java Sparrow rarely looks untidy or ruffled. Feather condition in this species indicates the state of health and ruffled feathers often suggest illness. If in doubt, consult your veterinary surgeon.

It is advisable to keep a Java Sparrow with birds of fairly average size such as weavers, whydahs and Cut-Throat Finches and not with small waxbills. In large aviaries, however, many fanciers do keep this species mixed with Zebra Finches and other similar birds.

There are now several colour forms of the Java Sparrow, the original grey and white, fawn and pied. The description below applies to the grey bird.

Description:
Size: 13 cm (5½ in)
COCK:
Head and tail: black. Cheeks: white. Body: dove-grey. There is an eye ring of red, bare skin. Beak: pink. Legs: pinkish-beige.
HEN:
Alike. Sexing cannot be done by appearance, so watch for display behaviour.

Diet: (Seedeater)
Mixed millets and plain canary seed form the basic diet. Hemp is also appreciated, as is greenfood. Grit and cuttlefish bone must always be available.

A pair of Java Sparrows

Breeding:
Boxes or baskets are often used.

(Diamond Sparrow, see page 75. Yellow Sparrow, see page 134.)

LAUGHING DOVE □ ◄
Streptopelia senegalensis   *in colour*
Origin: Africa   *page 95)*

A very suitable species for inclusion in a mixed collection, as it is a very tame dove, which is far more lively than most other types. It does not, however, agree with its own kind, so keep only one pair.

Description:
Size: 25 cm (10 in)
COCK:
Head, throat and chest: reddish-brown. Collar: black. Upperparts: reddish-brown, merging into grey. Stomach: white. Chin: white. Eyes: brown. Eyelids: red. Beak: black. Legs: red.
HEN:
Grey all over.

Diet: (Seedeater)
Mixed millets, oats and hemp, if available, form the basic diet. Occasional greenfood and a few insects are enjoyed, but these are not essential.

Breeding:
Pairs frequently choose a conifer as a nest site and build a rather messy nest from twigs and straw. Try to provide a wire mesh base to start off the construction.

Two eggs are laid and both cock and hen share in the incubation which takes 13 days. The cock feeds the hen at this time. When the two chicks emerge they usually prove to be a cock and hen. They are almost totally independent in a further 12 days and should then be taken away from their parents, as a new round is started immediately.

This species can produce up to five or six broods in one season, but more than five should not be allowed, or the hen may become exhausted and produce inferior chicks.

(Diamond Dove, see page 74.)

LAVENDER FINCH ●
Lagonosticta caerulescens   *(in colour*
Origin: West Africa   *page 22)*

This is a lively finch with quick movements, which makes a peaceful yet interesting addition to a mixed aviary. However, it also has a tendency to pluck its own feathers and also those of its companions. For this reason, it is recommended that only one pair of this species be kept. A lone pair do not pluck each other quite so readily as several kept together. This species becomes tame very quickly and has a quiet murmuring song, which is repeated quite frequently as it settles down to roost.

Description:
Size: 13 cm (5 in)

COCK:
Body: Grey. Rump: scarlet. Beak: dark grey. Legs: dark grey.
HEN:
Similar, but the grey plumage appears slightly muted and is often more smoky-brown in tone. The hen is slightly smaller.

Diet: (Seedeater)
Mixed millets form the basic diet. Greenfood, spray millet and some livefood such as fresh ants' eggs should be provided. Grit and cuttlefish bone must always be available.

This species needs protection from severe weather in an indoor flight but extra heat is not necessary.

Although it often looks very scruffy when offered for sale because of its habit of feather plucking, this should not deter a prospective buyer. It does not indicate poor health. Once installed in an aviary, the bird should soon improve.

Breeding:
A Lavendar Finch pair nests happily in a nest box with a small round entrance hole or in a globular wicker basket. Sometimes the birds build their own nest in a bush. Plenty of nesting material should be provided including soft grasses, moss, wool and feathers. The hen lays four to five round white eggs and incubation usually lasts about 12 days. The young fledge in 14 days.

Soaked seed, egg rearing food and soaked bread should be provided for rearing the young. Extra supplies of fresh ants' eggs should be given.

Occasionally the Lavender Finch hybridises with the Fire Finch, if housed in the same aviary. This produces a hybrid which is very attractive in appearance.

The Lavender Finch can be allowed free flight outside the aviary during the breeding season, once a nest has been completed, as it returns to feed its young.

LONG-TAILED GRASSFINCH HECK'S GRASSFINCH
Poephila acuticauda
Origins: North West Australia

Two forms of this beautiful bird exist: the Long-Tailed Grassfinch, which sports a yellow beak, and the Heck's Grassfinch, which has a coral beak. A bird with an orange beak is a cross or hybrid of the two types.

This bird can be aggressive and is best kept with Diamond Sparrows and Zebra Finches.

Description:
Size: 18 cm (7 in)
COCK:
Head: silver-grey. Body and wings: fawnish-grey. Belly: paler fawn. Oval bib on throat and upper breast: black. Eye stripe: black. Thighs: black and white. Tail: black. Beak: yellow, coral or orange as explained above.
HEN:
Similar, but often has a smaller black bib. This bird is quite difficult to sex by appearance.

Diet: (Seedeater)
Plain canary seed and mixed millets form the basic diet. Millet sprays and seeding grasses are eagerly consumed. Greenfood is accepted by some of this species, but ignored by others. Grit and cuttlefish bone must always be available.

Left: *a Long-Tailed Grassfinch* **Right:** *Heck's Grassfinch*

Although a fairly hardy species, it will fare better in cold weather if provided with some heat.

Breeding:

The cock bird displays by ruffling his bib whilst singing and performing a hopping jig before his intended mate.

This bird prefers to choose his own mate for breeding. Pair bonding between cocks and hens of this species is often for life and a compatible pair breed well if conditions are suitable. A colony may be kept with the other recommended species so that there is plenty of choice for partner selection.

Breeding should not be contemplated before the pairs are a year old. As the hen is susceptible to egg binding even when mature, it is advisable to add cod liver oil to her seed once a week to prevent this problem.

Nest boxes and baskets should be placed in the aviary in medium height bushes giving a variety of choice.

A little privacy will encourage the birds to commence nesting preparations. Some cover should be provided, with easy access. The nest will usually be lined with soft grasses, moss and feathers, so always provide plenty of nesting materials so that they will not fight over possession of favoured items.

Four to six white eggs are laid and incubation is shared by cock and hen with both parents roosting in the nest at night. The incubation period lasts 17 days. Nest inspection is not usually resented, but should be kept to a minimum. The young chicks are fed by their parents for 21 to 23 days.

During the rearing period, sprouted seed and extra millet sprays should be given. Bread and milk may also be fed,

but take care not to allow the milk to sour. Soft rearing food mixed with hard-boiled egg is eagerly taken, and some birds also enjoy chopped mealworms.

The young should be independent after a further month, and should be separated from their parents before further breeding. If birds are housed indoors, take the parents from the quarters and leave the young in the surroundings that they know. Some chicks have been known to refuse food and die after having been moved. If housed out of doors, it is easier to partition off part of the flight while further broods are raised.

The parents should not be allowed to rear more than three broods a year. As they attempt to breed all year round, cocks and hens should be separated after the third round. Split ring the progeny for future identification.

MAGPIE MANNIKIN
Amauresthes fringilloides
Origin: South Africa and West Africa

This attractive large mannikin is very hardy and can remain outside all year round. It should be housed with larger birds or those who are aggressive and able to defend themselves, since it can be quarrelsome and has a heavy beak which can inflict injuries. A well matched pair of Magpie Mannikins with similar markings often does well on the show bench.

Description:
Size: 10 to 13 cm (4 to 5 in)
COCK:
Head: black. Back, wings and tail: brown. Underparts: white. Beak: top mandible, black; lower mandible, grey. Legs: black.

A Magpie Mannikin

HEN:
Alike. May not be sexed by appearance, so it is best to purchase several birds and allow them to pair themselves.

Diet: (Seedeater)
Plain canary seed and mixed millets form the basic diet. Spray millet is enjoyed. Greenfood is appreciated by certain Magpie Mannikins, but ignored by others. Grit and cuttlefish bone are essential.

Breeding:
Several pairs may be housed together in a large aviary for breeding purposes, since they are colony breeders in the wild. Odd birds should be removed.

Pairs construct a nest in open-fronted nest boxes or globular wicker baskets. They use whatever materials are available, including grasses, leaves and twigs, forming an entrance passage into the nest.

Four to six eggs are laid and the birds take turns in sitting for the 12-day in-cubation period. Chicks may be reared on dry seed alone, but sprouted seed should be provided with extra millet sprays, chopped mealworms, ants' eggs and soaked stale bread.

The young commence their juvenile moult at around 12 weeks of age, but often do not attain full adult plumage until they are one year of age.

(Three-Coloured Mannikin, see page 129. White-Headed Mannikin, see page 133.)

MASKED GRASSFINCH ○ ■
Poephila personata   *(in colour*
Origin: Australia   *page 23)*

This attractive grassfinch spends a great deal of time on the ground and is sometimes a little less hardy than other species of grassfinch. However, it thrives well if provided with suitable accommodation with protection against damp and cold. Although not aggressive, except in the breeding season, this bird has a tendency to disturb its aviary companions with frequent alarm calls for no particular reason. It is not a good bird to exhibit, since it sits on the cage floor too frequently.

Description:
Size: 13 cm (5 in)
COCK:
Body: cream-grey. Wings: beige. Tail, mask and upper thighs: black. Beak: yellow.
HEN:
Very similar but a little paler in colour with a slightly smaller mask. The hen's beak is also a paler yellow. Behaviour is a more reliable indication to the sex of the bird, but the cock must be watched

carefully to spot the ruffling of his throat feathers and to hear his song.

Diet: (Seedeater)
Plain canary seed, mixed millet and finch tonic seed form the basic diet. Charcoal should always be available, for without this breeding is not attempted. Grit and cuttlefish bone are also necessary.

Breeding:
Standard half-open nest boxes should be provided at low levels. If several pairs are kept, they should be allowed plenty of space between nesting sites. Once the hen has accepted a nest box, it is 21 days until the first egg is laid. Progress is far slower than that of other grassfinches. The nest building is a lengthy affair with both parents taking part in lining the nest with moss and feathers. The normal clutch is five eggs, with cock and hen sharing the incubation and rearing of the chicks.

Masked Grassfinches tend to rear their young on one solitary type of food. Some parents feed only sprouted seed, others only standard canary rearing food mixed with hard-boiled egg or brown bread and milk. Some seek out livefood. Watch carefully to learn their preference and always provide larger amounts of the favoured dish until the young are independent. The juvenile moult commences when the chicks are nine weeks old. This species is sometimes rather aggressive during the breeding season.

Masked Grassfinches have hybridised on many occasions with the Long-Tailed Grassfinch, Parson Finch, Zebra Finch, Bicheno, Cherry Finch and Chestnut-Breasted Finch.

If difficulties occur in rearing young Masked Grassfinches, Bengalese may be used as foster parents.

NAPOLEON WEAVER
Euplectes afra afra
Origin: West Africa

A lively and active weaver, which can be aggressive during the breeding season.

Description:
Size: 10 cm (4 in)
COCK (in nuptial plumage, during the breeding season):
Head: thick yellow ruff. Back: yellow. Body: black and yellow. Wings: black and buff. Throat: yellow. Eyes: black. Beak: black. Legs: black.
HEN:
Alike, so it is not possible to sex bird by appearance outside the breeding season when both the cock and hen are light greyish-brown in colour.

When buying any type of weaver, look for bright eyes, a clean vent and well shaped legs and feet. Scruffy feathers are not a sign of ill health in this species, as it is a soft feathered bird and plumage is easily damaged.

Diet: (Seedeater)
Mixed millets and plain canary seed form the basic diet. Greenfood, grit and cuttlefish bone should always be available.

This hardy species may winter outside during the day, but should be provided with a dry, frost-proof shelter or unheated room at night.

Breeding:
A nest is constructed in a nest box, which should be provided. The weaver also uses old nests, vacated by other weavers, fashioned to its own liking.

Three to four eggs form an average clutch and incubation takes 12 days.

A Napoleon Weaver

Both parents take turns to sit on the eggs by day and roost in the nest box at night. Chicks fledge in three weeks.

During the breeding season the cock's display is really amusing to watch. He puffs out his feathers to display his yellow ruff to best advantage.

ORANGE-CHEEKED WAXBILL ●
Estrilda melpoda (*in colour page 19*)
Origin: West Africa

This is an attractive member of the wax-bill family, although this one can be rather timid and shy on occasion. It is very hardy once acclimatised and has rather endearing habits, one of which is wagging its tail from side to side when excited or frightened.

Description:
Size: 10 cm (4 in)
COCK:
Body: fawnish-brown. Head, crown, chin and throat: pale grey. Rump: crimson. Tail: black. Cheek patches: bright orange. Beak: red. Legs: greyish-cream.
HEN:
Very similar, but orange cheek patches are a little smaller.

Diet: (Seedeater)
Mixed millets and plain canary seed, spray millet, seeding grasses and some greenfood keep this species in excellent health. Grit and cuttlefish bone must always be available.

Breeding:
Pairs are not always very successful in breeding. They sit rather fitfully, often leaving the eggs if disturbed, and fail to incubate them properly. Favoured nesting sites are boxes, baskets or thick bushes in which a domed nest is constructed. Avoid disturbances.

Four eggs form the usual clutch and the incubation period is 11 days. Plenty of small livefood is necessary. Aphids, if available, or fruit flies, small smooth caterpillars and fresh ants' eggs are valuable food supplies. Soaked and sprouted seed is also very beneficial.

(Cordon Bleu, see page 73. Golden-Breasted, see page 79. Red-Eared, see page 120. Violet-Eared, see page 132.)

PAGODA MYNAH
Sturnus pagodarum
Origin: India and Sri Lanka

This small mynah may be kept outside all year round after acclimatisation and does not require a great deal of space. It is confident and bold and can be a little aggressive when kept in pairs. A single bird mixes well with other similar sized softbills, but keep a close watch on pairs to see no fighting occurs with other aviary inhabitants. A single bird becomes very tame with its owner. This engaging bird often imitates the call sounds of other birds with great skill.

Description:
Size: 20 cm (8 in)
COCK:
Head and crest: black. Face, neck and stomach: buff. Shoulders and wings: grey-blue merging into dark grey. Tail: dark brown with a white tip. Beak: yellow with a blue base beneath the nostril area. Legs: greenish-yellow.
HEN:
Very similar to the cock, but sometimes a little smaller with a shorter crest.

Diet: (Softbill)
Its diet is similar to that of the Andaman Mynah. Coarse grade insectile mixture should be combined with a wide variety of diced fruit. Livefood is necessary and berries, soaked raisins and sultanas are enjoyed. Raw beef can provide variety.

Breeding:
A large box or log situated in a quiet corner encourages this species to construct a rather untidy, large nest. A shelf in the bird room or shelter is often selected. A tame bird is inclined to build a more visible nest. Try to provide a variety of nesting material such as long grasses, mosses and feathers from the aviary.

A clutch of three or four eggs is normal. Mealworms and ants' eggs help in chick rearing.

(Andaman Mynah, see page 56. Rothschild's Mynah, see page 123.)

PEKIN ROBIN
Leiothrix lutea
Origin: China

The lively Pekin Robin fits into a mixed collection of birds including even small

A Pekin Robin

finches, but is sometimes intolerant of its own kind. Therefore, only a single pair or a cock bird should be kept in an aviary. Avoid keeping this bird in a collection where smaller birds are breeding as the Pekin Robin has a nasty tendency to rob the nests and eat the eggs. If breeding only birds of a larger size than the Pekin Robin the problem does not arise.

Since this bird loves to bathe, try to include a small pool in the aviary.

The Pekin is a hardy type and winters well, taking moults in its stride. It may be left outside provided there is a dry, frost-proof shelter available.

This bird is easily tamed.

Description:
Size: 15 cm (6 in)

COCK:
Body: brownish-green. Wings: brown with red. Eye: black. Eye ring: cream. Beak: orange. Breast: yellowish-orange. Legs: cream.
HEN:
Similar, but much duller. Try to listen for the melodious song of the cock as this is the best method of sexing this bird.

Diet: (Softbill)
Fine grade insectile mix, fruit, greenfood and about six mealworms per day form the basic diet. It also takes a little seed on occasions, if housed with seedeaters. This bird should be given a variety of insects as available. It has quite a small appetite.

Right: *A Pagoda Mynah*

Breeding:
Pairs construct a deep cup-shaped nest of reeds, bark, moss and fine small twigs. Linings of moss should be placed in the base of nest boxes. The boxes should be provided in a secluded position high up in dense vegetation. Between three to five eggs are laid and incubation last 13 days. The young fledge some 12 days after hatching. They are dependent on their parents for several further weeks.

PETER'S TWINSPOT ● ○ ■

Hypargos niveoguttatus *(in colour*
Origin: East Africa *page 26)*

This attractive bird requires careful acclimatisation and it should always be considered rather delicate, even when firmly established. It must be protected from sudden changes in temperature. A large aviary is not necessary, but a sunny position is preferred. It is pleasant natured and is very placid with other seedeaters.

Description:
Size: 13 cm (5 in)
COCK:
Head: brownish-grey. Back: reddish-brown. Neck, sides of head and chin: bright red. Upperparts: black with white spots on flanks. Wings: dark brown. Tail: black and red. Beak: black. Legs: cream to grey.
HEN:
Much less red on head, generally paler coloured and with fewer white spots.

Diet: (Seedeater)
A varied diet is necessary. Mixed millets, plain canary seed, spray millet and some livefood, including chopped mealworms,

fresh ants' eggs and a little greenfood, form the basic diet. Germinated seed and grass seed are relished. In cold weather and while breeding, stale white bread soaked in milk, egg food and a little cod liver oil help to keep this bird in good condition. Fruit is also enjoyed, particularly oranges. Grit and cuttlefish bone are essential.

Breeding:
The display of the cock bird prior to breeding is similar to that of the Green Twinspot. A pair usually constructs a nest in bushes a little off the ground. Box and dwarf conifers are favoured nesting sites. Nest boxes may be provided, although they make their own nests quite successfully using grasses and other material. A narrow entrance passage is constructed.

During the breeding season the cock chases other birds away from the nest site, but otherwise he is peaceful. The young hatch in 13 days and fledge in a further three weeks. The young should be fed chopped mealworms, egg food, soaked bread and germinated seed for quite some time. They should not be expected to thrive on hard seed alone for several months after leaving the nest.

(Green Twinspot, see page 89.)

PILEATED JAY △

Cyanocorax affinis
Origin: South America

As with many of the jay family, the Pileated Jay is inquisitive, active and something of a clown, and can become very tame. It may be housed with other large softbills, doves and pheasants, but

A pair of Pileated Jays

not when other birds are breeding as it often robs nests, taking eggs or chicks.

Description:
Size: 36 cm (14 in)
COCK:
Head: black. Throat and chest: black. Nape of neck: blue-white. Upperparts: brownish-blue. Belly: white. Moustache streak: blue. Beak: black. Legs: grey.
HEN:
Alike. Hard to sex by appearance, so observe behaviour.

Diet: (Softbill)
Coarse grade insectile mix mixed with minced beef forms the basis of the diet. The remainder of the menu should comprise mixed fruits, mealworms, maggots and some soaked raisins, sultanas and perhaps a little sponge. Mealworms are a great aid in taming. An occasional frozen dead chick or mouse should be fed thawed.

Breeding:
The Pileated Jay is a difficult bird to breed. Pairs are cautious about nesting and need plenty of seclusion and space. They may be provided with a well-covered open fronted nest box, but occasionally they may be tempted to construct their own untidy nest in a bush. Three to five eggs form the normal clutch and the incubation period lasts three weeks. Sadly they frequently devour their own young after they hatch. A plentiful supply of livefood, particularly small mice, may help to discourage this.

PIN-TAILED PARROT FINCH
○ ■
(in colour page 27)
Erythrura prasina
Origin: India and Indonesia

A rather timid and nervous bird that requires careful acclimatisation, but thrives well if given a little extra attention. Once established in a well planted aviary, it lives outside without any difficulty. It mixes well with other seed-eaters of similar size and is not aggressive, but needs plenty of space in which to exercise, as it has a tendency to get fat.

Description:
Size: 13 cm (5 in)

COCK:
Body: green. Face and throat: blue. Lower breast, tail and rump: bright red. Long pointed central tail feathers. Beak: black. Legs: cream.
HEN:
Similar, but no blue on face or red on lower parts. The hen also has a much shorter tail. The immature cock bird resembles a hen.

Diet: (Seedeater)
Plain canary seed and mixed millets form the basic diet. Greenfood and sprouted seed are enjoyed. Grit and cuttlefish bone are essential. This species often needs unpolished rice during the acclimatisation period as it sometimes refuses other food, but later canary seed often proves the favourite seed.

Breeding:
The cock bird performs a very interesting courting dance, circling the hen and jerking his tail up and down while uttering a few strange noises.

The nest may be built in a box, in a bush or under some form of cover. More than one pair of this species can be kept in a mixed collection, as fighting is unlikely.

Four to five eggs form an average clutch. The incubation period is 13 days and both parents take turns in sitting on the eggs. Try to provide plentiful supplies of soaked seed and a few mealworms and ants' eggs.

PIN-TAILED WHYDAH ○ ■ ◄
Vidua macroura
Origin: Central Africa

This is a very impressive and graceful member of the whydah family, however a

A Pin-Tailed Whydah cock

little care must be exercised when keeping this species in a mixed collection. A lone bird will not attempt to hurt or disturb small finches, but when there are several pintails there is only one way to ensure peace and harmony, and that is to keep just one cock bird and several hens.

If these measures are not adopted there will be a great deal of unrest and the species can be rather aggressive. If possible, the flight should be roomy. It is also wise to provide plenty of food dishes.

Description:
Size: 13 cm (5 in)
COCK: (in breeding plumage)
Length: 30 cm (12 in) including the tail where the four long central feathers measure from 18–25 cm (7–10 in). Forehead, nape and crown of head: glossy blue-black. Cheeks and throat: white with a white band around the neck. Upperparts: black with rump and upper-tail coverts white. Underparts: white. Black crescent on chest. Four central tail feathers black; flights black-brown. Beak: light red. Legs: dark grey. When not sporting the nuptial plumage the cock resembles the hen.
HEN:
Centre of crown of head: sandy colour. Sides edged in black. Mantle: buff striped with black-brown, together with scapulars. Rump: brown with striped markings. Flights and tail feathers: dark brown with buff edges. Throat: white. Underparts: buff mainly, darker on flanks and breast, often with darker markings. Beak: pinky-brown. Legs: light brown. Young birds resemble hens but their beaks are horn-coloured.

Diet: (Seedeater)
Mixed millets, spray millet, greenfood

and some apple form the basic diet. Grit and cuttlefish bone should always be provided. The cock bird has a long sweeping tail when in nuptial finery, and food dishes should be placed in high positions off the ground so that the one sole cock bird which should be kept in a mixed collection does not spoil his magnificent tail.

Breeding:
In their natural state, whydahs are parasitic breeders. The hen lays her eggs in the nest of a small finch, which incubates them and rears the young. Every whydah species chooses a certain type of finch for this purpose, whose young resemble its own chicks in feather colour and reflecting papillae (luminous markings in the roof of the mouth). The Pin-tailed Whydah most frequently lays her eggs in the nest of the St Helena Waxbill, *Estrilda astrild* or the Red-eared Waxbill, *Estrilda troglodytes*; both make excellent hosts for Pin-tailed Whydah young. As long as just one cock and, say, four or five hens are kept, it is well worth experimenting by keeping this species with suitable waxbills since this type of breeding is most interesting to observe.

You can, of course, keep just one Pin-tailed Whydah cock with a waxbill collection merely for the beauty of the bird in nuptial plumage.

(Yellow-Backed Whydah, see page 135.)

PLUM-HEADED PARRAKEET □
Psittacula cyanocephala (in colour
Origin: India and Sri Lanka   page 26)

This species may be housed with some of

the larger seedeaters, such as cardinals and other gentle natured parrotlike types, such as the Cockatiel. This species is hardy and remains outside all year round, if a frost-proof shelter is provided.

Description:
Size: 36 cm (14 in)
COCK:
Head: rose pink. Throat and neck ring: black. Upper parts: green. Breast: yellow-ish-green. Shoulder patch: dark red. Wings and tail show some blue and yellow feathers. Beak: orange-red. Legs: grey.
HEN:
Similar, but her head is blue-grey, her beak yellow and her body does not have the red shoulder patches.

Diet: (Seedeater)
Plain canary seed, mixed millets,

A Pope Cardinal (top centre)

sunflower seed, peanuts and a little hemp form the basic diet. This bird enjoys apple and plenty of greenfood. Grit and cuttlefish bone must always be provided.

Breeding:
Since young cock birds resemble adult hens, it is best to purchase a fully mature pair when hoping to breed.

Pairs usually breed best in separate accommodation but can be bred in a mixed aviary, if it is fairly large.

Nest boxes should be slightly larger in size than the normal budgerigar box, although some Plum-Head pairs use this size. Boxes should be hung fairly high with space left on top to allow the bird to sit and guard the nest. Nesting material should consist of sawdust and wood shavings. This should be provided in the base of the boxes.

Four to six eggs are laid which the hen incubates alone. She does not leave the nest until the eggs have hatched and the chicks are ten days old. The cock bird feeds the hen and chicks from the time the eggs are laid. Hard-boiled egg, soaked bread, ants' eggs, mealworms and soaked and sprouted seeds should be supplied.

Plum-Heads are shy breeders and abandon their nests if disturbed.

(Bourke's Parrakeet, see page 63. Red-Rumped Parrakeet, see page 121.)

POPE CARDINAL ◀ ◇
Paroaria dominicana
Origin: Brazil

This lively, attractive song bird resembles the Red-Crested Cardinal, but is better tempered, smaller and has no crest. It has a very melodious voice. It is not aggressive with similar sized birds, but a pair are shy of breeding in a mixed collection.

Description:
Size: 18 cm (7 in)
COCK:
Head and throat: bright red. Stomach: white, fading to grey. Back, wings and tail: dark grey. Beak: cream. Legs: dark grey.
HEN:
Identical, so it is difficult to select a true pair.

Diet: (Seedeater)
Plain canary seed, mixed millets and a little sunflower seed form the basic diet. If available, hemp seed is enjoyed. Some birds enjoy a little fruit. Greenfood and livefood should be given to breeding pairs and an occasional maggot or mealworm is appreciated out of the breeding season. Grit and cuttlefish bone must always be available.

This bird needs a large aviary with plenty of cover. It is hardy, but should be encouraged to use a shelter in cold weather as it has a habit of roosting outside. If not keen to use a shelter, try to provide some outside cover near the favourite perching and roosting spot.

Breeding:
As pairs are nervous and shy, it is better to remove the birds to a separate quiet area for breeding. The hen chooses her mate carefully, so it is advisable to purchase several birds and allow natural pairing. Its nesting habits are much the same as the Red-Crested Cardinal.

An artificial nest site should be provided at shoulder level. An untidy nest is constructed from grasses and heathers, if available. A willow basket often proves a

A Purple Glossy Starling

popular nesting site as do thick bushes.

Four to six eggs are laid and both parents take turns in incubation and feeding. Plenty of livefood should be provided, together with hard-boiled egg and fresh ants' eggs. When the young fledge, they should be fed the same diet.

(Green Cardinal, see page 85. Red-Crested Cardinal, see page 119.)

PURPLE GLOSSY STARLING ○ ■
Lamprotornis purpureus
Origin: Africa except north

An extremely beautiful member of the starling family, it is frequently kept mere-ly for its beauty and the fact that it can be easily tamed. However, a word of caution must be given: while it is feasible to keep a single bird with other species in a mixed collection, a pair should always be housed alone. It is sometimes possible to keep a pair with others that are larger than themselves but a careful watch should be maintained. As with most birds there are exceptions to every rule; you can come across peaceful types in any species, but it is always wise to be cautious.

Description:
Size: 20–22 cm (8–8¾ in)
COCK:
Head and underparts: violet-purple.

Wings and back: metallic glossy green and blue. Tail (which is short): violet. Beak and legs: black. Eyes: golden yellow.

HEN:

Very similar but slightly smaller than the cock.

Diet: (Softbill)

Coarse grade insectile mix, fruit and livefood, fed every day, form the basic diet. All fruit should be chopped up into cubes. Worms, mealworms and chopped raw meat are enjoyed by this species. Minced beef may be blended with the insectile mix. Raisins, sultanas and currants are appreciated. All ingredients can be mixed together and provided in one dish. This species is a greedy feeder.

Breeding:

Supply a pair with a large nest box with an entrance hole near the top. Provide plenty of nesting materials including hay, dried grasses and roots. If you are lucky, a large untidy nest is constructed, completely filling the nest box. Three to four eggs are laid. The incubation period is normally 13 days. A great deal of livefood must be provided when there are young in the nest. Maggots, smooth-backed caterpillars and wood lice may be given. Chicks should be segregated from their parents as soon as they are able to feed themselves, or they may be attacked when a second round of eggs is laid. One of the more successful starlings at captive breeding, this species has also cross-bred with other types of starling. To have the best chance, however, one pair of Purple Glossy Starlings housed alone is best.

A single cock bird would look impressive with other similarly sized birds and such species as the White-crested Laughing Thrush (*Garrulax leucolophus*) seem to agree well with starlings, perhaps because they can all be fiery tempered. Sudden outbursts of bad temper do occur with starlings and such events can prove fatal.

(Superb Spreo Starling, see page 128.)

PURPLE SUGARBIRD
Cyanerpes caeruleus (in colour page 18)
Origin: Guyana

The Purple Sugarbird is one of the most attractive and brightly coloured of the sugarbird species. It is a delicate bird and must be carefully acclimatised. The Purple Sugarbird may be kept as a single pair with other small softbill or seedeating species. Several cock birds may be kept together with other birds. Do not keep more than one pair of sugarbirds with their own kind or other species, because fights may occur.

An indoor aviary in winter is a must and heat is required. In warm summer months, this sugarbird lives happily outside in a planted flight. It can live in captivity for 10 to 12 years under the right conditions.

Description:

Size: 13 cm (5 in)

COCK:

Body: purple-blue. Ear coverts: black. Wings, throat and tail: black. Beak: black. Legs and feet: yellow with black claws.

HEN:

Body: green. Throat: chestnut. Underparts: pale yellow with green markings. Throat has pale violet blue moustache markings at sides. Lores: chestnut. Beak:

dark brown. Legs and feet: greenish-brown.

Diet: (Softbill)
Diet should be as varied as possible. Fine grade insectile mix should be fed together with a wide selection of fruit, including oranges, bananas and pears. It likes to feed on fruit suspended on stout thread near perching spots, which keeps the food clean and minimises fouling by droppings. Water mixed with just enough honey to colour it should be supplied in drinkers positioned well above ground level. Mealworms, fresh ants' eggs, hard-boiled egg mash, cooked mashed potato and boiled rice mixed with honey are all enjoyed. Stale, soaked bread, sponge cake or rusks may be crumbled into a honey and water mix.

Breeding:
This species is not easy to breed. Nests are made of plant fibres suspended in tall bushes and a well planted conservatory may encourage a pair to go to nest.

Two or three small, white eggs are laid. The incubation period may vary between 14 and 21 days.

Moulting normally occurs twice a year, although cocks have been known to go an entire season without moulting.

(Yellow-Winged Sugarbird, see page 137.)

RED AVADAVAT ●○
Amandava amandava
Origin: India, Sri Lanka and Malaysia

This bird is an excellent choice for a novice fancier. It is attractive and pleasantly disposed to other birds. It is willing to breed in an aviary, away from aggressive birds. The cock bird's song is delightful although short.

Description:
Size: 10 to 13 cm (4 to 5 in)
COCK:
Beak: red. Wings: dark brown. Sides and breast spotted with white. Body: bright red. Tail: black. Legs: brown. This is the only waxbill that has an eclipse plumage outside the breeding season, when the brightly coloured cock bird moults to resemble the drab coloured hen.
HEN:
Beak: red. Body: dark brown with beige on abdomen. Wings: spotted with white. Upper tail coverts: red. Black stripe on ear coverts. Legs: brown. (Immature cocks look like hens.)

Diet: (Seedeater)
Mixed millets and spray millet are enjoyed. Plain canary seed should be provided in a separate container. Green food and seeding grasses are also relished, and grit and cuttlefish bone must be available.

This waxbill winters successfully outside without heat, needing only a frost-proof shelter. It survives healthily for many years outside in a planted aviary where the plumage retains its beautiful red colour better than if housed inside.

Breeding:
The cock bird performs a prancing courtship dance displaying his spread tail.

This bird makes use of a wicker basket or builds its own nest in dense shrubbery. It does not like to breed in enclosed boxes as much as other small finches. The hen lays between four and six eggs which she incubates, without assistance from the cock, for around 12 days. When the

A pair of Red Avadavats

chicks hatch, the parents should be given small live insects, sprouted seeds and seeding grasses to feed them with.

This species shows a strange preference for using black chicken feathers to line the nest, arranged in the form of a screen. The provision of such feathers by a thoughtful owner encourages nesting, as do Box bushes. This bird builds its hanging, pouch-shaped nest inside the bush sometimes with two entrances.

RED-BILLED QUELEA ○ ◀ ◇
Quelea quelea
Origin: Africa

This species is a very suitable weaver for novice fanciers. If several pairs are kept, Budgerigars, Cut-throat Finches or Zebra Finches make suitable companions. One single pair is safe with smaller finches if the accommodation is fairly large.

Below: *a Red-Billed Quelea*

Description:
Size: 10 to 13 cm (4 to 5 in)
COCK:
Body: golden-brown with dark brown markings. Face: chocolate brown. Beak: red. There is a red rim around the eye. Legs: pinky-brown. The plumage of the cock bird turns dull after the breeding season.
HEN:
Has a pale yellow beak.

Diet: (Seedeater)
Mixed millets, spray millet and plenty of insect food and half-ripened grain, such as grass seed, form the basic diet. Grit and cuttlefish bone must always be available.

This hardy bird can be kept in an outside flight all year round. However, ensure that the bird roosts in a shelter when moulting from nuptial plumage.

Breeding:
This bird is particularly difficult to breed. However, the cock is a very keen nest builder and is normally assisted by his mate. A ball-shape nest is constructed with an entrance at one side. Fresh grass is the preferred nest material, so new grass clippings should be provided. Pairs often build one nest, destroy it and then rebuild a new one right next to the first.

This weaver is a colony nester, so several pairs of birds may be kept to encourage breeding attempts. Despite the fact that pairs build plenty of nests, very few reports exist of successful captive breeding, so this bird presents a challenge to the keen fancier. Fighting it not likely unless the aviary is very small.

A Red-Crested Cardinal

RED-CRESTED CARDINAL ◄ ◇
Paroaria cucullata
Origin: South America

A striking bird, it is bold and confident, good for exhibiting and tames quite easily.

Description:
Size: 20 cm (8 in)
COCK:
Crest: red. Body: grey and white. Eyes: black. Legs: black. Tail: black.
HEN:
Similar, but slightly smaller and slimmer. The only sure indication of sex is the cock's rather attractive song during the breeding season.

Diet: (Seedeater)
Plain canary seed and mixed millets form the basic diet. It also enjoys a little plain sunflower seed. Insectile mix, mealworms and fresh ants' eggs are eagerly devoured. Grit and cuttlefish bone must always be available.

This bird lives happily in most temperatures, but may often be seen basking in a patch of sunlight on the ground. A frost-proof shelter should be provided.

Breeding:
Nesting takes place in untidily built nests about knee high from the ground. These are built in thick bushes or hedges. Heather and grass blades are often used for nesting material. Willow or wicker baskets can be used as a base.

Both parents share the incubation of the eggs and rearing of the young. Four to six eggs form a normal clutch. Hard-boiled egg may be added to the normal diet for rearing. This species appreciates plentiful livefood when breeding and will eat small smooth-backed caterpillars, maggots, locusts and woodlice. Spiders are often enjoyed.

When first leaving the nest the chicks have ginger coloured crests. The young birds are sometimes fed at ground level after fledging and the chicks flutter their tail feathers while wittering for attention. The Red-Crested Cardinal is usually a very protective parent.

Once mature, this species has a tendency to put on weight. So provide a large flight to prevent it becoming lazy and taking insufficient exercise.

(Green Cardinal, see page 85. Pope Cardinal, see page 113.)

RED-EARED WAXBILL ●
Estrilda troglodytes
Origin: Central Africa

A lively and tolerant waxbill, this bird is easy to keep in a mixed collection.

Description:
Size: 10cm (4 in)
COCK:
Body: pinkish-beige. Wings: light brown. Tail: light brown. Eye stripes: red. Beak: red. Legs: cream. The cock assumes a pink colour on the belly during the breeding season.
HEN:
Similar, rather difficult to sex by appearance. Observe behaviour and look for pink colour on belly of cock.

Diet: (Seedeater)
Mixed millets and plain canary seed form the basic diet. Millet sprays and seeding grasses are relished. Greenfood, grit and cuttlefish bone must always be available.

The Red-Eared Waxbill is quite hardy but should have a frost-proof shelter or room for winter. When moulting, this bird needs a little extra attention and warmth, plus a few drops of cod liver oil.

Breeding:
The Red-Eared Waxbill should be encouraged to nest when there are plentiful supplies of fresh ants' eggs available for chick rearing.

The cock dances around his hen with a blade of grass in his beak. He has a 'chirrupy' mating song. The hen often replies with a soft, quiet, gurgling sound.

If breeding, this bird requires a secluded corner of the aviary as it is easily frightened off the nest. Nesting boxes should be provided. The nest is constructed with a narrow entrance passage and lined with hair and wool, which should be placed on bushes near the nest site for the bird to pick up. A choice of boxes fixed at varying heights encourages this bird to breed.

The hen lays between three and five white, pointed eggs and the incubation period lasts between 11 and 22 days, both parents taking it in turn to sit on the eggs.

Fresh ants' eggs, egg food and soaked and germinated millet seed should be fed to the parent birds.

The chicks are ready to leave the nest 14 days after hatching. The fledglings are pale grey in colour with black beaks. A few weeks later they assume adult plumage.

This waxbill has on many occasions

A Red-Eared Waxbill

bred with the Orange-Cheeked Waxbill, Golden-Breasted Waxbill and the Crimson-Rumped Waxbill, producing attractive, unusually marked birds.

(Cordon Bleu, see page 73. Golden-Breasted, see page 79. Orange-Cheeked, see page 104. Violet-Eared, see page 132.)

RED-RUMPED PARRAKEET ☐
Psephotus haematonotus
Origin: Australia

This is one of the most popular species of Australian parrakeets, because it is hardy and simple to feed, and therefore easy to keep. Breeding results are normally good. However, take great care when attempting to keep this species with other birds, as it can be very spiteful. If in doubt, keep a pair alone. In any case, it is best to have only one pair in a mixed collection.

Description:
Size: 28 cm (11 in)
COCK:
Body: varying shades of green. Stomach: yellow. Wings: edged with dark blue. Rump: red. Beak: black. Legs: grey.
HEN:
Does not have the red rump and is less distinctive in colour. Beak: grey.

Diet: (Seedeater)
Plain canary seed, mixed millets, sun-flower, hemp (if available), groats and oats form the basic diet. This species enjoys greenfood and loves apple. Grit and cuttlefish bone must always be available.

A spacious aviary is required with a dry, frost- and damp-proof shelter for bad weather. Plenty of wing exercise is important.

Breeding:

For those fanciers inexperienced in breeding birds, the Red-Rumped Parrakeet is a good choice, as pairs require the minimum of supervision. A pair nests very readily if a large nest box is provided. Rotting wood should be placed in the base to a depth of 10 cm (4 in).

A normal clutch of eggs numbers between four and seven. The incubation period is 21 days with the hen sitting alone. The parents rear their young with very few additions to the normal diet, but try to provide soaked and sprouted seeds.

The young fledge in one month and may be left with the parents for a further two or three weeks until the hen begins another round. They should be removed at the first sign of this, or the cock may attack the fledglings.

(Bourke's Parrakeet, see page 63. Plum-Headed Parrakeet, see page 111.)

A pair of Red-Rumped Parrakeets, one of the most popular species of parrakeets among aviculturists. This species is easy to keep and usually easy to breed. A pair of these birds requires a roomy aviary and they are often best kept alone.

ROTHSCHILD'S MYNAH ◆ △
Leucopsar rothschildi
Origin: Bali

This truly beautiful softbill is sometimes called a mynah, a starling or a grackle, which can be rather confusing. It is very attractive, easily tamed and simple to feed. It may be housed with other similar sized softbills with safety.

Description:

Size: 25 cm (10 in)
COCK:
Head (including crest): white. Body: white. A wide area of blue-green bare skin surrounds eyes, covers lores and extends to sides of neck. Beak: creamy-grey. Legs: pale grey. Black tips on wings and tail.
HEN:
Similar, but smaller and slimmer.

Diet: (Softbill)

This species enjoys proprietary brand mynah pellets. Diced fruit of all kinds should be given and may be coated with coarse grade insectile mixture. Raw meat is also appreciated.

This hardy bird thrives in a large aviary with a shelter which does not have to be heated. It can withstand quite low temperatures. It loves to bathe and takes a great pride in its appearance, regularly grooming its white feathers.

Breeding:

Plenty of cover should be provided to encourage pairs to make an attempt at breeding. Although few captive breedings have been recorded, there is evidence that this species does go to nest if the conditions are suitable.

A selection of nest sites should be available including boxes, logs and large baskets filled with straw. Livefood is necessary if young are produced.

(Andaman Mynah, see page 56. Pagoda Mynah, see page 105.)

A Rothschild's Mynah

SPICE BIRD ● ○ ■
Lonchura punctulata   *(in colour*
Origin: India and Sri Lanka   *page 94)*

The Spice Bird is one of the most popular of the mannikin family. Hardy and easy to manage, it is an ideal species for the novice fancier.

Description:
Size: 13 cm (4½ in)
COCK:
Head: chocolate brown. Upperparts: brown. Underparts: white and each feather is edged with dark brown. Beak: grey. Legs: brownish-grey. Eyes: black. Tail: dark brown.
HEN:
Alike, so sexing cannot be done by appearance. Listen for the unusual buzzing, humming song of the cock bird. If possible, purchase several birds to encourage them to select their own mates.

Diet: (Seedeater)
Plain canary seed and mixed millets form the basic diet. Millet sprays and greenfood are also enjoyed. Grit and cuttlefish bone must always be provided.

It can be housed outside throughout the year and only requires a dry, frost-proof shelter for roosting during winter.

Breeding:
Spice Birds are not particularly keen breeders, but do go to nest under the right conditions. Nest boxes and wicker baskets should be provided in secluded places, such as shrubberies. Pairs make their own nests inside boxes or baskets with soft grasses, mosses and feathers. They desert their nests at the slightest noise or disturbance.

A Spice Bird

Four to eight eggs are laid and the incubation period is 13 days. The parents should be kept well supplied with sprouted seeds, millet sprays, greenfood and insects.

Should a pair fail to try to rear their young, Bengalese may be used as foster parents. Bengalese often interbreed with this species. They come from the same family (*Lonchura*). Parent-reared Spice Birds may be kept with their family to form a small colony.

SPLENDID GRASS PARRAKEET ☐
Noephema splendida
Origin: Australia

This parrakeet is peaceful and tolerant even during the breeding season and may safely be housed with Bourke's Parrakeet and/or the cockatiel, although it is keener to breed if kept on its own. It is much sought for its beautiful colours.

A Splendid Grass Parrakeet cock

Description:

Size: 23 cm (9 in)

COCK:

Head: Deep blue. Upperparts: green. Stomach: yellow. Chest: red. Wings: green with blue and black feathers. Tail: green with black and yellow feathers. Eyes: brown. Legs: blackish-brown. Beak: black.

HEN:

No blue on head or red on chest. Underside: olive green, and brown above.

Diet: (Seedeater)

Plain canary seed, mixed millets, sunflower seed and oats form the basic diet. Greenfood and apple are appreci-ated. Grit and cuttlefish bone must always be available.

A spacious aviary with a dry, frost-proof shelter should be provided, with protection from harsh winds.

Breeding:

Large nest boxes, slightly deeper than those liked by budgerigars, should be placed in the quarters. Pairs are usually quite eager to go to nest.

A clutch of eggs may number up to seven. The incubation period is 19 days and both parents share in sitting and rearing. When the young fledge they resemble the hen. Young cock birds soon sprout a few red feathers around the base of the neck and some blue on the head. Two rounds of eggs per breeding season are acceptable.

(Elegant Grass Parrakeet, see page 77. Turquoisine Grass Parrakeet, see page 130.)

STAR FINCH ● ○ ■
Bathilda ruficauda
Origin: Northern Australia

This is a popular Australian finch which is quite easy to breed. It is a peaceful species. During the breeding season, a pair may be transferred to separate accommodation.

Description:
Size: 13 cm (4½ in)
COCK:
Body: olive green. Breast: olive. Underparts: pale yellowish-green. Forehead: red. Cheeks and throat: red. Tail: brick red. Face and breast spotted with white dots. Beak: red. Legs: flesh.
HEN:
Similar, but less red on the face. It is sometimes easy to mistake a young cock bird for a hen, if it has not attained full colour, so it is wise to try to obtain a mature, known pair for breeding.

Diet: (Seedeater)
Small plain canary seed and mixed millet form the basic diet. Greenfood and seeding grasses are enjoyed. Grit and cuttlefish bone must always be available.

As the Star Finch does not roost overnight in a nest box, it should be protected from cold and damp weather conditions. Bathing is enjoyed, so a pool should be provided, if possible.

Breeding:
A young hen often flies over her intended mate with a piece of grass in her beak, sometimes dragging it over his back. This is considered to be a preliminary ritual to pair bonding.

Star Finches like to build their own nests in broom bushes interwoven with hay, but they do accept a nest box or a wicker basket, in which they will construct a dome-shaped nest of grass with a narrow entrance hole.

Pairs should not be allowed to breed until they are fully mature at two years of age. If a hen lays fertile eggs prior to this age, they may be placed under Bengalese.

Egg binding is sometimes a problem with Star Finches, particularly if the weather is cold. They are also inclined to leave the nest frequently instead of sitting on the eggs full time, so it is often better to place the pair in a flight by themselves to minimise disturbance.

Three to four round white eggs form the normal clutch and both parents incubate them during the day, although the hen usually sits for longer periods than the cock. Both birds occupy the nest at night. The eggs hatch in 12 to 14 days and the young are covered in fine white down. Star Finches are very attentive parents and do not seem to resent nest inspection, although this should always be kept to a minimum. The chicks leave the nest at 18 to 23 days and appear to be very shy at this stage. Three or four weeks later they should be independent and removed from their parents to allow for a further round. Immature birds are pale olive brown with a little red in the tail.

The juvenile moult occurs at between six weeks and eight months of age depending on how quickly the young mature, weather conditions and diet.

A Normal Star Finch cock

Although chick rearing pairs can be fed on hard seed alone, they benefit from sprouted seed, egg rearing food and insects.

A very strong pair bond is formed by Star Finch couples, so they should be rung with split plastic rings to make sure they are always kept together.

SUPERB SPREO STARLING △
Spreo superbus *(in colour*
Origin: East Africa *page 30)*

This is one of the most popular and beautiful of the glossy starling species. It has a very discordant cry, so is most often kept for its fabulous colour and ease of taming. It is a good exhibition species. Whilst a single bird does not harm those of other species, a pair can be spiteful and murderous. A pair kept for breeding needs to be kept in a separate flight. This species likes to bathe, so provide a pool in the aviary, if possible.

Description:
Size: 20 cm (8 in)
COCK:
Head: blue. Back: green. Chest and stomach: chestnut. Upper breast: blue. A white band separates these two colours.

Beak: black. Legs: black.
HEN:
Alike. This species cannot be sexed by appearance, so observe behaviour.

Diet: (Softbill)
Coarse grade insectile mix, fruit and livefood fed every day form the basic diet. All fruit should be chopped up into cubes. Raisins, sultanas and currants are also enjoyed. Minced raw beef should be blended with the insectile mix, and all ingredients can be mixed together in one dish.

Breeding:
Supply a pair with a large nest box with an entrance hole near the top. Try to give plenty of nesting material including hay, dried grasses and roots. A large untidy nest is built completely filling the nest box.

Three to four eggs are laid and the incubation period lasts for 13 days. Plenty of livefood is required, including mealworms, maggots, smooth backed caterpillars and woodlice.

Chicks should be segregated from their parents as soon as they are able to feed themselves, or they may be attacked when a second round of eggs is laid.

(Purple Glossy Starling, see page 114.)

THREE-COLOURED MANNIKIN ○ ■
(Tri-coloured Nun)
Lonchura malacca
Origin: India

The Three-coloured Mannikin is very easy to manage, but not a bird from which to expect spectacular breeding results. It is a very popular species with beginners since it is so hardy. Most of the mannikin species share this quality. They are all simple to keep.

Description:
Size: Just under 10 cm (4 in)
COCK: and hen are alike.

A pleasing colour combination of black, white and chestnut-brown. Cannot be sexed by appearance.

Diet: (Seedeater)
Mixed millets and plain canary seed form the basic diet. Spray millet, seeding grasses and greenfood are enjoyed. Grit and cuttlefish bone must always be available.

Breeding:
Breeding this species is a challenge for the fancier. It is worth making the effort to try to create the type of conditions this species would find in the wild. Just to give you an idea, in India their habitat would be in long grass, mostly near rice fields where the nests would be built, hanging from the sturdy stems. Therefore, you could use bamboo or ordinary cane or rushes planted in the flight with other shrubs. It is worth trying to encourage the birds to nest. The provision of a few old nests might be worth trying; sometimes this species will take over an old nest and rebuild. Small livefood should be provided, together with fresh ants' eggs, and some mashed hard-boiled egg may be fed. Stale soaked bread and germinated seed should be made available if you find yourself with a nest of chicks.

This species has no audible song but it has a most attractive, glossy appearance and usually does well on the show bench.

Plenty of different types of mannikins are available but this is certainly one of

A Three-Coloured Mannikin

the best. It is a very healthy bird which usually thrives with the minimum of attention. It is well worth persevering in attempting to breed with this species.

(Magpie Mannikin, see page 101. White-Headed Mannikin, see page 133.)

TURQUOISINE GRASS PARRAKEET □

Neophema pulchella

Origin: New South Wales, Victoria and South Australia

(in colour page 30)

This brightly coloured parrakeet is easy to manage, feed and breed. It may be kept with other parrotlike species, such as Bourke's Parrakeet, if the aviary is fairly large. It becomes active in the evening, but is quiet and lethargic during the day. It needs plenty of flying space. A frost-proof shelter is required for bad weather.

Description:
Size: 20 cm (8 in)
COCK:
Body: green. Lores and cheeks: turquoise-blue. Throat and chest: yellow. Wings: blue and chestnut red. Beak: horn colour. Legs: yellowish-grey.
HEN:
Similar, but duller colours. No chestnut red on wings. Less blue on face.

Diet: (Seedeater)
Mixed millets, plain canary seed and sunflower seed form the basic diet.

Greenfood and a liberal quantity of maw seed are appreciated. Soaked and sprouted seeds should be fed at all times. Grit and cuttlefish bone must always be provided.

Breeding:
The courtship display of the cock includes a soft whistling song. Nest boxes should be provided for breeding pairs and they often use a budgerigar nesting box. The base should be filled with damp moss or wood pulp.

Four to five eggs are laid and the hen incubates alone. The incubation perod is 17 to 19 days. The cock bird feeds her while she is sitting and for a further few days after the chicks have hatched. Both parents then feed the young. Rearing food should include soaked and sprouted seeds, soaked bread, greenfood and maw seed. Young birds should not be allowed to breed until they attain two years of age.

(Elegant Grass Parrakeet, see page 77. Splendid Grass Parrakeet, see page 125.)

VINACEOUS FIRE FINCH ●○
Lagonosticta larvata vinacea
Origin: West Africa

A very peaceful waxbill, similar to the African Fire Finch, that agrees readily with others and is very attractive. This species may be housed in quite a small aviary with other small seedeaters, but must have extra warmth in cold weather.

Description:
Size: 10 to 13 cm (4 to 5 in)
COCK:
Head: dark grey. Black stripe above

A Vinaceous Fire Finch

beak, across eyes and cheeks. Throat: black. Back, breast and stomach: wine red. White spots on sides of breast. Underparts: black. Tail: dark red. Wings: brown. Beak: grey.
HEN:
Body: greyish-brown with a red cast. Stomach: pinkish-beige. Head: light grey.

Diet: (Seedeater)
The basic diet consists of mixed millets, spray millet, soaked and sprouted seed, chopped mealworms and insects as available. Grit and cuttlefish bone must always be available.

Breeding:
Pairs go to nest quite readily, building a round nest from available materials, such as soft grasses and mosses.

Three to five eggs are laid which hatch in 11 days. Both parents share in the incubation. Try to provide fresh ants' eggs, chopped mealworms and mashed egg yolk. Dried ants' eggs should be soaked in warm water prior to feeding.

VIOLET-EARED WAXBILL ●○
Granatina granatinus *(in colour*
Origin: West and South Africa *page 23)*

Try to gain experience with other, more easily managed waxbill types before keeping the Violet-Eared Waxbill. Although its feathers are rather soft in texture, a bird in good condition exhibits well. Only one pair should be kept in a mixed collection, since the cock is aggressive with other cock birds of his own kind, although tolerant of other birds.

Description:
Size: 13 cm (5 in)
COCK:
Body: dark rich brown. Forehead and rump: deep violet blue. Underparts: chestnut. Cheeks: violet. Tail: black. Beak: red. Legs: black.
HEN:
Similar, but lighter on head, back and underparts. Cheeks: very pale violet, so this bird can be sexed fairly easily. Hens are often in short supply.

Diet: (Seedeater)
The Violet-Eared Waxbill must have a daily ration of insects, ants' eggs, grubs and mealworms. Mixed millets and plain canary seed, millet sprays and some greenfood should also be provided, and grit and cuttlefish bone must always be available. Try to provide as varied a diet as possible.

This species needs extra care in cold weather and sometimes a little extra warmth. It should be protected from sudden changes in temperature.

Breeding:
The cock bird has a very pleasant song

reminiscent of the lark. The hen also sings, but very softly.

Breeding is difficult: a secluded spot in which to nest and a very varied diet are required. This is one of the few waxbills which must have insect food, even outside the breeding season. Greenfood, such as chickweed, dandelion and groundsel, is useful when breeding. Seeding grasses, mashed hard-boiled egg, cheese, grits, charcoal, finely grated ground egg shells are necessary too. Try to encourage this bird to take fine grade insectile mix.

Three to four eggs are laid and incubation takes 12 to 14 days. The young fledge in three weeks, resembling the hen in appearance. On maturity, at around three months of age, the sexes can be identified. Otherwise, nest building and preparation is the same as with other waxbills.

(Cordon Bleu, see page 73. Golden-Breasted, see page 79. Orange-Cheeked, see page 104. Red-Eared, see page 120.)

WHITE-CRESTED △
LAUGHING THRUSH
Garrulax leucolophus
Origin: India

A bold, amusing bird which is very entertaining in a large aviary. It may be mixed with other starlings and thrushes, but should not be housed with smaller types or very timid birds. It is also rather noisy.

Description:
Size: 30 cm (12 in)
COCK:
Back: chestnut-brown. Wings and tail:

A White-Crested Laughing Thrush

darker brown. Head, crest and chest: white. Face: sports a black mask. Beak: black. Legs: gun-metal grey.

HEN:
Similar, making it difficult to pick a true pair, although its crest is smaller than that of the cock.

Diet: (Softbill)
Coarse grade insectile mixture and raw minced beef should be fed two or three times a week. Livefood is also necessary. Mixed fruit of all kinds should form about 40% of the menu, and insectile mixture should be sprinkled over diced fruit.

This species becomes very hardy after acclimatisation and can be kept outside, needing only a dry, frost-proof shelter, free from damp and draughts. It often attempts to roost outside even in cold weather, but should be discouraged from doing so.

Breeding:
Few successful breeding results have been

recorded, but this should not deter the keen fancier from trying. Try to provide a secluded aviary and plenty of livefood for rearing the young.

WHITE-HEADED MANNIKIN   ○ ■
Lonchura maja
Origin: Indonesia

This bird is hardy enough to be kept outside all year round and frequently lives for over ten years. Even when breeding, this species is tolerant and peaceful with other seedeaters of similar size and habits, and its ease of management makes it an excellent choice for the beginner.

Description:
Size: 13 cm (5 in)
COCK:
Body: chocolate brown. Head: white. Beak: greyish-blue. Legs: grey. Eyes: black.
HEN:
Similar, but the head and beak are smaller than those of the cock.

Diet: (Seedeater)
Mixed millets and greenfood form the basic diet. If available, an occasional mealworm is enjoyed. Grit and cuttlefish bone must always be available.

Breeding:
It is sometimes a little difficult to get pairs to start breeding, but once accomplished, this bird rears young very well. An average clutch is four eggs with an incubation period of 12 days.

Rearing food should be provided in the form of soaked bread and a few chopped mealworms, if available, together with the normal seed diet. The young fledge in 25 days and the parents continue to feed them for some time afterwards. This species is often cross-bred with Bengalese.

(Three-Coloured Mannikin, see page 129. Magpie Mannikin, see page 101.)

A pair of White-Headed Mannikins

YELLOW SPARROW

Auripasser luteus
Origin: East Africa

This hardy, brightly coloured bird is very easy to manage and feed. It may be kept outside all year round, but must not be

mixed with small finches as it can be aggressive. It agrees well with Java Sparrows, mannikins and some of the smaller weavers.

Description:
Size: 13 cm (5 in)
COCK:
Head: yellow. Back: chestnut. Wings: brown. Tail: brown. Stomach: yellow. Beak: cream, turns black during breeding season. Legs: brown.
HEN:
Head: buffish-brown. Mantle: buffish-brown. Stomach: buff and yellow. Beak: cream.

Diet: (Seedeater)
Mixed millets and plain canary seed form the basic diet. Millet sprays and green food are enjoyed. It also appreciates some live-food, particularly small smooth caterpillars and mealworms. Grit and cuttlefish bone must always be provided.

Although a very active bird, it does spend a great deal of time out of sight in dense vegetation, if such cover is provided in the flight.

Breeding:
This is a difficult species to encourage to breed and plenty of cover is needed. Nest boxes and wicker nest baskets should be provided, sited low down in dense foliage to tempt pairs to start nest building. A large untidy nest is constructed, which is dome-shaped with a side entrance. Gorse bushes often prove popular sites. Pairs only go to nest if left strictly alone, so do not inspect the nest.

Three to four eggs form a normal clutch, which the hen incubates alone. The incubation period lasts around 16 days. Both parents share in rearing.

A Yellow Sparrow

Plenty of insects are necessary when young are in the nest. These should include small smooth caterpillars, small beetles and mealworms. Greenfood and plentiful supplies of sprouted seeds must also be made available when the adults are feeding chicks.

(Diamond Sparrow, see page 75. Java Sparrow, see page 97.)

YELLOW-BACKED WHYDAH
Coliuspasser macrourus   *(in colour*
Origin: West Africa   *page 90)*

This whydah has a beautiful yellow back when in breeding plumage. It is lively, alert and unaggressive with birds of similar size and habits.

Description:
Size: 20 cm (8 in) in breeding plumage. 14 cm (6 in) at other times.

COCK:
Body: black with some brown edging on wings. Shoulders and mantle: bright yellow during breeding season. Beak: black. Legs: dark brown. When not breeding the cock moults to resemble the hen.

HEN:
Slightly smaller and dull brown. Chin and throat bear a yellowish tinge. Stomach: white with brown streaks.

Diet: (Seedeater)
Plain canary seed, mixed millets and seeding grasses form the basic diet. Livefood and spray millet are appreciated. Greenfood is consumed occasionally, but not every bird enjoys it. Grit and cuttlefish bone must always be available.

A roomy aviary should be provided with a dry shelter for roosting. This species often tries to roost outdoors so it must be encouraged inside if the weather is damp. Low temperatures are not harmful, but wet weather can cause illness.

Breeding:
This whydah is not a parasitic species, but is polygamous: breeding is encouraged if each cock bird has several hens. Unfortunately, it is not always easy to obtain hens.

The male bird builds the nest himself, using dried grass and small roots. The hen lines the nest with any soft material she can find, including feathers. She continues lining the nest even after the eggs are laid. By the time the young are ready to leave the nest, it is usually very solid.

The cock does not share in incubation and rearing. He can be quite spiteful, often chasing and annoying the hen. Usually three or four eggs are laid and incubation takes 13 days.

(Pin-Tailed Whydah, see page 110.)

YELLOW-COLLARED IXULUS ◆
Ixulus flavicollis
Origin: Himalayas
(in colour page 31)

A small, drab coloured bird which is lively, inquisitive and amusing to observe.

Description:
Size: 10 cm (4 in)

COCK:
Body: dark olive brown. Nape of neck: yellow. Chest and belly: greyish-white. Crest: dark brown. Beak and legs: brown.

HEN:
Identical, so this bird cannot be sexed by appearance. Cock birds are aggressive in defence of their territory chasing off larger birds very actively, and their behaviour is the best way of determining sex.

Diet: (Softbill)
Ixulus often take a nectar mixture of honey and water to excess and ignore other essential nutrients. Their diet must be carefully monitored. Soft fruit such as pears, grapes and berries should be provided together with fine grade insectile mix and small live insects. Sponge cake soaked in honey and water is enjoyed. Houseflies and blowflies are eagerly devoured, but maggots and mealworms

often prove too tough skinned for this small species.

This bird must be carefully acclimatised and needs housing in a warm conservatory in cold weather, as it tends to be rather delicate.

Breeding:

This is a difficult species to breed. Accommodation with plenty of cover is needed to encourage breeding. Preferred nesting sites are similar to those chosen by the Black-Chinned Yuhina. Shrubs and climbing plants with fine grasses and roots are used for nesting material.

A Yellow-Winged Sugarbird cock

A maximum clutch numbers three eggs and the incubation period is around 16 days. Plenty of small livefood is necessary for rearing the young.

YELLOW-WINGED SUGARBIRD
Cyanerpes cyaneus
Origin: South America

This beautiful softbill is quite hardy once established and, like the Purple Sugarbird, it is sometimes called a honeycreeper. It can live for many years if given the

correct type of care. A single pair agrees well with other small birds, but if several sugarbirds are kept, they should all be cock birds. If a hen is introduced, fights occur.

Description:
Size: 10 to 13 (4 to 5 in)
COCK (in nuptial plumage):
Body: bright cobalt-blue. Shoulders, wings, tail: black. Head: turquoise blue on crown. Beneath the wings is an area of yellow. Legs: red. The cock bird moults twice a year.
HEN
Varying shades of olive green. Legs: creamy-brown. When not in nuptial plumage, the cock resembles the hen, but can always be distinguished by his red legs.

Diet: (Softbill)
As with the Purple Sugarbird, fine grade insectile mixture forms the basic diet. Fruit, such as pears, bananas and oranges, should be provided. Grapes, sultanas and raisins are relished. Large fruit should be suspended on a thread near a perch. Honey and water must be provided in a drinking tube.

This bird may be kept in an outdoor aviary when properly acclimatised, but is seen to best advantage in an indoor room setting (examples of which are shown in Chapter 1). It needs extra warmth in cold weather, and should not be submitted to extremes of temperature at any time. It loves to bathe.

Breeding:
To encourage breeding, a pair must be provided with suitable nesting material in the form of soft grasses and mosses. The nest is most often constructed in a dense bush fairly high off the ground.

Two to three eggs are laid and the incubation period is 13 to 14 days. Plenty of small livefood is necessary for rearing.

(Purple Sugarbird, see page 115.)

ZEBRA FINCH
Poephila guttata
Origin: Australia

The Zebra Finch is an ideal species with which to begin bird keeping.

There are several different forms of this domesticated species. The description below is for the original colour.

Description:
Size: 13 cm (5 in)
COCK:
Body: grey. Underparts: buff and white. Ear patches: bright chestnut. Flanks: chestnut, spotted with white. Throat: black and white barred. Beak: red. Legs: orange.
HEN
Similar, minus throat markings, chest barring, lobe and flank markings. Beak: paler red than the cock bird.

Other colour forms available are fawn, white, isabel, pied, silver-winged, and albino.

Diet: (seedeater)
Plain canary seed and mixed millets form the basic diet. Dry seed alone keeps this species in excellent health. Millet sprays should be given as a treat and greenfood may be provided. Grit and cuttlefish bone must always be available.

Breeding:
Zebra Finches nest in boxes or wicker

A Normal Zebra Finch cock

baskets, which should be well packed with nesting material by the owner. A small space should be left to allow the pair to finish off their nest. This prevents them from making 'sandwich nests', when eggs are laid in an empty box or basket and then another nest is built on top.

Zebra Finches are very inquisitive and often inspect other birds' nests. If they are intent on their own nesting, however, they are less inclined to make a nuisance of themselves in this way.

Zebra Finches lay many eggs and attempt to breed at any time of the year. They should not be allowed to breed too frequently as the hens become exhausted. It is best to allow a pair to rear only two nests of chicks per season. Segregate cocks and hens to prevent overbreeding.

Six eggs form an average clutch and eggs are laid on consecutive days. The incubation period usually begins after the second or third egg. One or two chicks hatch a couple of days after the rest. Both parents share in incubating the eggs and feeding the chicks. Wholemeal bread and milk, soaked seed and canary rearing food should be provided.

Chicks leave the nest around 20 days of age. Any young birds which are slow in learning to feed themselves should be encouraged with millet sprays, which they find easier to manage. The parents may often be seen feeding their young on the ground at this stage.

As soon as they are independent, young stock should be removed from their parents and the cocks segregated to prevent them from attempting to breed before they are fully developed.

GLOSSARY

Aviary Accommodation for keeping birds either in or out of doors.
Aviculture Keeping of birds in captivity.
Bobhole Entry hole in shelter.
Brood Group of chicks in the nest.
Cere Small patch devoid of feathers above the beak of certain birds, e.g. budgerigars.
Chick Infant bird.
Clear egg Infertile egg.
Closed ring Aluminium closed ring for fitting on leg of chick to prove it is owner bred and to record its age.
Clutch Eggs laid by a hen in one sitting.
Cock Male bird.
Coverts Feathers above the secondaries on the wings and those above the long tail feathers.
Crop Area of the throat where food is ground up with grit the bird has swallowed.
Dead-in-shell Chicks that do not develop properly and die before hatching.
Domesticated Species that has been consistently bred in captivity for many generations.
Down Fluffy layer beneath quills.
Egg binding Hen's inability to lay an egg.
Fancier Person who enjoys the hobby of bird keeping.
Feather plucking Removal of feathers by a bird, either its own or those of companions.
Fledgling A young bird emerging from the nest for the first time.
Flight Exercise area for birds usually constructed with wire netting or mesh.
French moult Disease causing unnatural loss of wing and tail feathers, most often experienced when breeding budgerigars.
Hand rearing Rearing of chicks performed by fancier if birds refuse to feed their young.
Hen Female bird.
Hybrid Result of crossing two different species, or of well marked varieties within a species.
Incubation Period of time after the last egg is laid until the chicks hatch.
Juvenile moult First moult of young birds.
Moult Feathers drop out and are replaced by new ones.
Mule Result of crossing a canary with a British finch.
Mutation Chromosomal change of colour or character.
Nuptial plumage Unusual colour of long feathers sported by cock birds only during the breeding season.
Pair bonding Cock and hen choose each other as mates, often for life.
Pied Bird whose colour is interspersed with light areas.
Pin feather Feather still encased in its sheath.

Plumage Collective term used to describe both quill feathers and down.

Preening Grooming of feathers by birds to distribute oil from the gland at base of tail. Birds also preen each other.

Quill Main shaft of a feather.

Seedeater Bird which lives on a diet of seed.

Shelter Enclosed part of aviary for roosting.

Softbill Bird which lives on a diet of fruit, insects, nectar, meat or multi-ingredient insectile mixtures, or a combination of these.

Split rings Coloured plastic rings which may be fitted on the leg of a bird of any age for identification.

Steady Term for a confident and calm bird.

Vent Anus.

INDEX

Illustrations are indicated in bold type